Robert Irwin Answers Questions About Penny Stocks

- How to win in this low-investment/high-yield market
- Where to find the stocks that sizzle!
- Ways to specialize in mining and energy stocks
- How to play a stock—when to get in, and when to get out!
- What to look for investment advisors
- How to win with new issues

Robert Irwin is the author of over a dozen very successful books on real estate, management, and personal finance, including *Wealthbuilders* and *Winning Strategies*. He lives with his wife, Rita, in Thousand Oaks, California.

Profits from PENNY STOCKS

AN INVESTOR'S GUIDE TO LOW-COST STOCKS & COMPANY START-UPS

Robert Irwin

BERKLEY BOOKS, NEW YORK

This publication contains the author's opinion on the subject. It must be noted that neither the publisher nor the author is engaged in rendering investment, legal, tax, accounting, or similar professional services. While investment, legal, tax and accounting issues in this book have been checked with sources believed to be reliable, some material may be affected by changes in the laws or in the interpretations of such laws since the manuscript for this book was completed. Therefore, the accuracy and completeness of such information and the opinions based thereon are not and cannot be guaranteed. In addition, state or local tax laws or procedural rules may have a material impact on the recommendations made by the author, and the strategies outlined in this book may not necessarily be suitable in every case. If legal, accounting, tax, investment, or other expert advice is required, one should obtain the services of a competent practitioner. The publisher and author hereby specifically disclaim any personal liability for loss or risk incurred as a consequence of the advice or information presented in this book.

This Berkley book contains the complete
text of the original hardcover edition.

PROFITS FROM PENNY STOCKS

A Berkley Book / published by arrangement with
Franklin Watts

PRINTING HISTORY
Franklin Watts edition published 1986
Berkley edition / October 1987

For information address: Franklin Watts,
387 Park Avenue South, New York, NY 10016.

ISBN: 0-425-10344-7

A BERKLEY BOOK ® TM 757,375
Berkley Books are published by The Berkley Publishing Group,
200 Madison Avenue, New York, NY 10016.
The name "BERKLEY" and the "B" logo
are trademarks belonging to Berkley Publishing Corporation.

PRINTED IN THE UNITED STATES OF AMERICA

10 9 8 7 6 5 4 3 2 1

CONTENTS

Profits from PENNY STOCKS

AN INVESTOR'S GUIDE TO LOW-COST STOCKS & COMPANY START-UPS

INTRODUCTION TO PENNY STOCKS

How would you like to buy a stock that costs just one cent? That's right, the full price per share is just a penny. Think of it—for a hundred dollars you could own ten thousand shares. For five hundred dollars you could own fifty thousand shares. And for a thousand-dollar investment, you could own a hundred thousand shares!

Of course, you may be thinking, "So what if it's cheap? So are bottle caps—the usual reason is that they aren't worth anything. If that's the case, what am I going to do with thousands of shares, paper my bathroom walls?!"

But wait; what if within a few months that penny-a-share stock you purchased was now selling for three cents a share—a 300 percent increase? Your hundred-dollar investment was now worth three hundred dollars. Your five-hundred-dollar investment was worth fifteen hundred dollars and your thousand-dollar investment was now up to three thousand dollars. Hardly the sort of thing that you'd use to paper walls.

Sure, you may be saying. Once in a great while a stock might go up 300 percent. But how realistic is that? After all, what we're talking about here is a threefold increase. That's like having IBM go from a hundred dollars (or wherever it currently happens to be) to three hundred dollars. It happens, but the chances are probably so remote as to be minuscule.

Don't bet on it. Let's go back to that one-cent stock. As it turns out, there are plenty of low-priced stocks that go up 300 percent in a short time. In 1985, for example—which in general was a bad year for low-priced stocks—scores of them did it. They had names like *Seburg Phonograph* or *Midas Gold* or *Metcom* or *NTN Communications* or a dozen others. The names can go on and on.

What's really interesting, however, is that the stock I was thinking of when I wrote the first few paragraphs of this introduction wasn't any of these. Rather, it was a controversion stock called *Nastech Pharmaceuticals*.

Nastech came out in April of 1984 at a cent a share. Within a few months it was up to three cents a share. By the end of 1985, it was at $1.25 a share.

That's right, $1.25! It only went up $1.24 in price, but that amounted to an increase of 125,000 percent!

If you had bought just $100 of Nastech when it came out, by the end of 1985 your stock would have been valued at $12,500. If you had purchased $500, your stock would have been valued at $62,500, and if you had stuck in the less than enormous sum of $1,000, you would have had a bundle valued at $125,000!

Certainly, for a stock to go up by that much doesn't happen every day. But it does happen, and Nastech isn't the first or the last low-priced stock to have it happen. (Prices can also go down. Nastech had plummeted back below fifty cents a share by the time this was written!)

In the world of penny stocks, big changes in value are commonplace. For example, let's take those stocks I mentioned earlier besides Nastech. Here's what their increases were during 1985:

STOCK	TIME FRAME	INCREASE	ORIGINAL COST
Seburg Phonograph	11 months	500%	$.25
Midas Gold	12 months	550%	$.20
Metcom	6 months	2,200%	$.01
NTN Communications	11 months	4,000%	$.20

Remember, these are just a fraction of the stocks that showed such increases. There are dozens that have also done as well. And probably thousands that have at least gone up somewhat in price. In fact, the penny stock market is loaded with success stocks. (It's also loaded with failed stocks. We'll see ways to avoid these in future chapters.)

BIG PROFITS—LITTLE PUBLICITY

This, of course, is the big reason that people invest in penny stocks—the chance to make a fortune. It's hard to find an individual who would turn down the opportunity to double, quadruple, or more his or her money in a short time. (Of course, that's not to say this market is without risk. As we'll see, both the rewards and the risks can be substantial.)

Yet, if you call up the average broker (one who handles stocks in general, not one who specializes in this field) and ask him or her about penny stocks, the chances are probably nine out of ten that the broker will suggest (perhaps insist) that you stay away from the pennies. I've heard brokers say, "It's a place where you can get hurt," or "The market is manipulated," or "You'll just lose all the money you put in."

The criticism of this field can also come from high places.

Louis Rukeyser, the host of the *Wall Street Week* television show and perhaps the most listened-to authority in stocks, suggests, "Don't buy a stock just because it's cheap. . . . Playing with low-priced stocks is a dangerous game that requires extra-strong information about the company and its prospects. It's not a safe game for beginners, who are all too apt to buy junk in the mistaken belief that its price makes it a bargain." (From *How to Make Money in Wall Street,* Doubleday Dolphin, 1976 edition.) By the way, the book is *must* reading for any beginner in stocks.

If Mr. Rukeyser and others of experience and reputation say low-priced stocks are bad, must not they be?

To these criticisms I would reply, yes, there's some truth in each of them. Yet, people still invest, and many of those investors do reap fortunes—as in any other field, from high-priced stocks to real estate to commodities. There are those who win and those who lose.

I personally think it is possible to profit in pennies, if you avoid the risks and the pitfalls. However, at the onset it's important to understand that this is not a field for the faint of heart or those who don't relish a challenge. There's money to be made here, but you do have to educate yourself and be willing to take a chance. (We'll have more to say about the psychology of the investor!) However, you don't need a lot of money to get started. In fact, that's another of the big appeals of this field.

THE REASON PEOPLE INVEST IN PENNIES

1. The Chances Are Greater for a Big Jump in Price in Low-Priced Stocks.

This should be obvious. If you have a hundred dollars to spend and you have a choice between buying a stock that sells for a hundred dollars a share or one that sells for ten cents a share, which is more likely to take a *big* price increase?

Most people will opt for a lower-priced stock. Here's why. Let's say that both stocks go up ten cents in value. With the high-priced stock you now have one share worth $100.10. You've made one thin dime. With the lower-priced stock you now have a thousand shares worth twenty cents apiece, or $200. You've made $100. The mathematics make it appealing.

Ah, but that comparison's not fair, I hear a Big Board (New York Stock Exchange) broker saying. It's easy as pie for a hundred-dollar stock to go up ten cents; after all, we're only talking about a .10 percent increase. But it's very hard for a ten-cent stock to go up ten cents. That's a doubling, or a 100 percent increase. In the long run, so this reasoning goes, you'll still make out better with the higher-priced stock.

Maybe, but to my way of thinking, it's a lot easier for *any* stock to go up ten cents a share (doubling the lower-priced stock) than it is for any stock to go up a hundred dollars a share (doubling the higher-priced stock). It's simply because a hundred dollars is so much more money than ten cents.

2. It's More Psychologically Appealing to Buy a Low-Priced Stock.

Everyone knows this, including the major corporations. People simply prefer stocks that are lower in price. That's why whenever a corporation's stock gets high, the company orders a "split." They issue two shares for one, or some such fraction, in order to get the price down to where investors will feel comfortable buying it.

After all, if this weren't really the case, then some stocks would be up there at a thousand dollars a share or higher.

(IBM or Xerox without splitting would be good examples.) Yet, except for some privately held companies, this almost never happens.

For a stock to be marketable, it must be low enough in price to appeal to investors. After all, only the largest institutional investors today can afford 1,000 shares of a stock costing over $100 a share. At $20, many more investors can own 1,000 shares. And at twenty cents, almost anyone can.

It's all a matter of how low is low. Is $20 the threshold of investor psychological appeal? Or $10? Or ten cents?

It's in the psychology of it. Would you rather own two or three shares of a high-priced stock or two or three hundred shares of a low-priced one? If you're the sort who would opt for the two or three shares of high-priced stock, then perhaps you'd best reconsider investing the time reading this book. On the other hand, if owning a lot of shares in what is undoubtedly a riskier company, but one with the potential to double or more in value, appeals to you, read on!

3. "It's One Gamble I Can Afford to Lose!"

A great many low-priced stock investors have no illusions about the market. They know it's a gamble and they know that the odds may be against them.

Nevertheless, they also know that even if they don't happen to hit it big, they won't get hurt too bad. They make sure that they don't invest more money than they can afford to lose. (Of course, as in any investment, the sky's the limit as to what you can put in.) Maybe it's only a few hundred dollars. Perhaps it's a thousand. But these investors know they can get into the market without a lot of cash. And they restrict their investment to just the amount they know won't hurt them in case things don't work out.

If they don't hit the long shot, well then, they'll sustain the loss and try again some other time. It's not like playing the Big Board, where you may need five thousand dollars just to get a round lot order (a hundred shares), or commodities, where the minimum margin may be three to five thousand dollars, or even real estate, where just a 10 percent down payment (which is what's realistic in today's market) can be ten thousand dollars.

Here you can put up less and lose less. Remember, at ten cents a share, investing a hundred dollars gives you a thousand shares. How bad can a person who owns a thousand shares for a hundred dollars get hurt? If the stock goes to zero, you're still only out a hundred bucks.

4. "It's a Long Shot That Could Make My Fortune!"

As those who play the pennies know, when dealing with stock that costs under a dollar a share, we're dealing with companies that are high risk. In most cases the chances of failure are far greater than the chances of success.

Nevertheless, a good many of these companies do succeed against the odds. And when they do, if you're holding their stock, you reap the benefits. You might lose on two, three, or more penny stocks before you hit it big. But if you do hit it, you could make your fortune on one stock. That's the long shot that holds the allure for this field.

IT'S UP TO YOU

What would you rather do? Go into your stockbroker's office and consider a stock that, if it does very well, might go up 25 percent? Or consider a stock that, if it does very well, might go up 10,000 percent! If you'd consider the latter, then you may be ready to try a fling at the pennies.

ARE YOU READY FOR PENNY STOCKS?

■

There was a time when the way to win in stocks, almost guaranteed, was to buy the "blue chips."

Blue-chip stocks, so called probably as a reference to the highest-priced blue chips at a poker table, were those that might not necessarily grow the fastest, but that would indeed continue to pay a strong dividend year after year.

Twenty years ago, in the 1960s, the bluest of the blue were the utility stocks. Everyone needed electricity. The country's growth was a certainty and the utilities would grow with it. Moody's (the rating service) maintains a utility stock average. In 1965 it hit a top of 120. Most people felt this was only the beginning.

Brokers in those days were urging "widows' and orphans' funds" (the euphemism for money you can't afford to gamble with and must preserve) to go into utilities. They offered "guaranteed" high dividends and "guaranteed" growth.

Many investors seeking security and reward opted for the utility stocks. They bought public power all over the country. Then they put their stocks in their safe-deposit boxes and forgot about them, confident they had made a wise and safe investment.

Of course, as anyone who really has invested in utilities knows, things didn't quite work out as planned. By the mid-1970s the utility average was down under fifty. Recently, after much struggling, it has only been able to get close to the nineties. As of this writing, it still isn't at the peak it achieved over twenty years ago.

What happened? Ask the investors in companies such as Washington Public Power Supply System. The utilities (many of them) invested in the future—nuclear power. Only, the costs of nuclear power were grossly underestimated and the productivity of that source of energy widely overrated. The utilities lost money.

Today many brokers consider utilities to be high-risk speculative issues. Yes, some still pay high dividends, right up until the day they default, like WHPSS. Utilities are hardly in the class of blue-chip stocks.

Of course, the utilities aren't the only casualties. There's the classic case of U.S. Steel, once considered the solid rock of blue-chip stocks. Beset by high costs and foreign competition, it turned out to be a true paper tiger.

Even high-tech blue chips have not worked out as many anticipated. Just a few years ago Apple Computer was considered one of the newest, brightest high-tech stocks—a new blue chip. Then it ran into that brick wall called IBM and its stock plummeted.

Of course, there is always IBM. But with the inroads in computers that the Japanese are making, can we still be sure?

I hope the picture is clear. Today most people realize that there is no such thing as a sure bet in stocks. The days of the blue chips are long gone. *All* stock investing today is inherently risky.

WHAT SHOULD YOU RISK?

My goal is *not* to convince you to take "widows' and orphans' " money and stick it in penny stocks. My recommendation is that you *do not* risk even 10 percent of your total investment money in pennies. What I do suggest, however, is that you do give this field a chance. Compare it with other investments. You may be surprised.

Of course, you should only make an investment after consulting with your own personal financial adviser. Even then you should only invest money that you are fully prepared to lose.

Just remember, we aren't necessarily talking big bucks here. This is a field where a hundred dollars can buy as much as 10,000 shares of stock.

ARE YOU THE RIGHT PSYCHOLOGICAL TYPE?

A final word needs to be said here about psychology and the market. When people talk about "gaining experience" and "learning the market," what do they really mean?

What they are talking about is not "book learning" or the gathering of information on stocks. Rather, what they are in truth speaking of is learning about themselves.

I've tried a wide variety of investments, including real estate, stocks, precious metals, and others. Along the way I've learned a few things about myself.

MY OWN EXPERIENCE

For example, I can still vividly remember the first time I invested in commodities. I bought a contract (just one) for gold. In commodities an individual can buy "long," betting the price will go up, or "short," betting it will go down. I bought long, anticipating the price would go up.

I only put up $3,500 as margin. However, at the time gold was $520 an ounce and my contract was for $52,000. For every dollar an ounce gold went up, I would make $100. For every dollar an ounce gold went down, I would lose $100. While the sky was the limit as to what I could make, if the price of gold plummeted by some horrible twist of fate all the way to zero and I couldn't get out of the market (which occasionally happens), I potentially could lose as much as $52,000!

Since I was convinced gold would go up in price, I wasn't worried . . . until that night.

Suddenly, from a deep sleep I sat bolt upright. I looked at my clock. It was 3 A.M. "My God," I asked myself, "what if I lose $52,000?!"

Never mind that the chance of losing that full amount was so remote as to be virtually impossible. It was the thought that held my mind. And I couldn't get back to sleep.

First thing the next morning, I called my broker. Gold had slipped $5.00 an ounce. I had lost $500. "Sell!" I shouted into the phone.

He unfortunately followed my instructions. I took my loss. However, within days the price had jumped $50 an ounce. If I had held, I would have made a $4,500 profit.

"KNOW THYSELF IN LOVE, WAR, AND IN MONEY"

I had lost at the market, but I had learned about myself. At that time in my life, I simply didn't have the temperament to risk more money than I put up. I left commodities (to return some years and a lot of experience later) and tried penny stocks.

Here the potential rewards were as great if not greater than with commodities. *But I only stood to lose what I initially invested.* If it put up $500 (assuming no margin), that's the most I could lose.

When I bought pennies, even though in some cases I might lose all the money I invested, I could still sleep peacefully at night.

WHAT IS YOUR COMFORT LEVEL?

How about you?

What is your comfort level in an investment? Is it similar to mine? Does knowing that you can't lose more than you have invested allow you to sleep at night? It might not.

There are some people I know who can't stand to lose any money at all. I have a friend, Jim, who is like this.

When Jim makes an investment, he wants to see a profit from the very first moment. If he buys a stock at $1.00 a share, he expects it to go to $1.10 the next day. If he buys real estate, he expects price appreciation immediately. If for any reason the price drops below his initial investment (the stock goes to ninety-nine cents or the real estate fails to appreciate), he gets apprehensive and nervous. He begins to think he's made a bad move. So he sells.

Needless to say, Jim doesn't get involved in many investments. In fact, right now he's got all his money tied up in certificates of deposit at banks. With a CD you start making money the moment you put your money in and it continues making money as long as it's deposited, often guaranteed (for what that's worth) by the U.S. government. Jim feels it's a no-lose situation.

Of course, he's only making 6.5 percent interest as of this writing. So it's not much of a win situation, either.

The point is, Jim has found an investment that fits his comfort level. He should never invest in penny stocks (where he might lose all the money he puts up) and certainly not in commodities (where he could lose more than his initial investment).

IT'S BETTER TO SLEEP AT NIGHT

What's your comfort level?

Are you a big risk taker?

Are you willing to lose a buck to make a buck or more?

Or do you like to hold your cash in your hand, where you can see and feel it all the time?

You really need to know. Finding out isn't a frivolous exercise. To succeed in penny stocks, you have to be willing to risk losing some money. If you're the sort who isn't comfortable doing that, then this chapter has more than just paid for the cost of this book. It's just saved you countless sleepless nights. Forget about penny stocks and run (don't walk) with your cash down to the bank and get a CD. You'll sleep easier, be healthier, and—even if you never get rich—probably live longer.

On the other hand, if you can take the heat, read on. Your fortune's waiting to be made.

WHERE PENNIES AREN'T (A LOOK AT THE TRADITIONAL MARKETS)

■

Where do we buy penny stocks?

That's a question I'm frequently asked, and if you're a traditional stock investor who hasn't bought pennies before, I'm sure you're also interested to know. Where are these elusive low-priced penny stock bargains to be found? After all, when we ask a traditional stockbroker about pennies, he or she usually gives us a scratch of the head and says, "There just aren't many out there worth considering."

Nonsense! There are hundreds, thousands out there. However, to find them we have to be willing to move beyond what most investors (particularly neophytes) consider the "traditional markets." This can be quite confusing, especially if you're new to penny stocks. So in this chapter we are going to set the stage. We're going to examine the traditional markets such as the New York Stock Exchange and the American Stock Exchange (called AMEX). Then, once we have firmly grasped what these are and how they operate, we'll move on to the exciting world of pennies.

First, let's define what a penny stock is.

WHAT IS A PENNY STOCK?

In the marketplace a penny stock is normally considered to be any stock selling for under $5 a share.

Of course, that's not a rule carved in granite. It's arbitrary, but it's widely accepted, so we might just as well go along with it. By this definition a stock that sells for $4.90 a share is just as much a penny stock as one that sells for ten cents a share.

Stocks for under $5 a share can be found in virtually any market. There are some (very few) on the New York Stock Exchange, the much smaller American Stock Exchange, and the various other smaller exchanges around the country. But most frequently we will find stocks for under five dollars in the "over-the-counter" or OTC market. It is here that we will primarily be looking.

Before getting to the OTC market, let's be sure we understand why we won't be looking for low-priced stocks on the Big Board and its various cousins.

THE NEW YORK STOCK EXCHANGE

The New York Stock Exchange is the largest and, without a doubt, most prestigious exchange in the world. It traces its origin back to the very founding of the country. It has the top companies listed (more than 2,000 of them).

It's important to understand at the outset that the Big

Board, as it is affectionately called, is not itself a buyer or seller of stocks. Rather, it is a marketplace where those who buy and sell come to conduct their business.

Those who buy and sell are said to have "seats" on the board. These individuals are usually officers or board members of large stockbrokerage firms, and they buy and sell stocks on an "auction" basis.

STOCK AUCTIONS

One of the more confusing things that newcomers to low-priced stocks get involved with is how the stocks are traded. Since the Big Board uses auctions, many neophytes believe that this is how all stocks not only are, but *should be*, traded. To avoid this problem, let's take a look at how an auction works so that when we get to the OTC market, we'll know the difference and be ready for it.

The vital thing to understand about auctions is that they are handled by *brokers*. Brokers representing various stock houses are on the floor executing their clients' orders. When you or I want to buy a Big Board stock, we go to our local stockbroker and explain what we want. Our request is phoned in to the floor man for the firm who, acting for us, finds another broker acting for a seller. A sale is then made.

It's not quite that simple, but the principle holds true. In an auction, stocks are continuously being exchanged, and their price is determined by supply and demand in an open market environment.

Of course, there has to be a little grease to keep the wheels of the market moving along smoothly, and this is provided in several ways. One way is by "odd lot dealers," who will buy orders for under a hundred shares. (A hundred shares, or a "lot," is the minimum order many brokers will handle.) These odd lot dealers essentially buy for themselves and then resell at a markup, thus explaining why there is sometimes a markup on less than a hundred shares. (Today, many large brokerage firms handle odd lot sales internally as a convenience for their clients.)

But the largest part of the lubricant that keeps the Big Board going is the "specialist." Specialists are located at various places on the floor of the exchange, and they "make a market" in a particular stock. It's important to understand that a specialist is a *dealer.* He buys and sells stocks for himself. He is dealing in the stock.

THE SPECIALIST

The specialist is needed because at any given time, there might not be enough buyers and sellers of a stock to keep an open auction going . . . or the buy prices and the sell prices might be so far apart that the market in a stock could come to a grinding halt.

Because he is committed to making a market in a given stock, at such times the specialist steps in and buys or sells so that there is always an open market for an issue. That is why he is called a "market maker." In theory, he buys when most others want to sell and sells when most others want to buy.

There have been countless articles and books written on how specialists may or may not manipulate the market. That's not really our concern here since we're only dealing with the Big Board in passing. However, it's important to note these concerns because when we get to the OTC market, we'll see a striking similarity between specialists and OTC dealers.

LISTED STOCKS

In the past the goal of many a board chairman was to get his or her stock "listed" on the Big Board. Besides prestige, it meant an entrée to the capital markets of the world. (This is changing today as many companies opt for other markets.)

Getting listed on the Big Board, however, is rather difficult. The New York Stock Exchange has strict requirements, such as insisting that the company show strong earning power (in the millions of dollars annually, going back several years), that it have enough shares to provide an open trading arena (usually a million or more), and that the total value of the company as measured by the value of the shares of stock outstanding be substantial (usually in the tens of millions).

Obviously, relatively few companies are going to have the qualifications to be listed here. And those that are listed are going to be quite substantial, meaning the value of their shares will probably be high, usually higher than $5 a share. (Finding stocks that are listed is an easy matter. Just check the financial section of any major newspaper, or if that fails, the *Wall Street Journal*. All Big Board stocks and their recent prices are given there.)

This, then, is the first reason we are not going to be looking for low-priced stocks on the New York Stock Exchange. There simply are not many there.

DOWN-AND-OUT

There are, however, occasionally some stocks listed on the Big Board that do indeed sell for under five dollars a share. In most cases we are going to be very skeptical of these.

My experience has been that low-priced stocks on the Big Board are from companies that are on the rocks. Usually stocks will come onto the Big Board at a price of at least $10 a share. Thus, if they are under $5, too often they are down from earlier levels and they may be on their way out. In other words, they are the losers.

For one reason or another, I have found that often a low-priced stock on the Big Board signals a company that is floundering. Of course, it could make a comeback, in which case buying the low-priced Big Board stock would be smart. (Good examples of just this are Wickes Co., which dropped to around $4 during its reorganization, then bounced back, and Sharon Steel, which dropped to fifty cents.) Most of the time, however, it hasn't worked that way for me. Too often, these companies just hang around for a while until they are "delisted."

DELISTING

When a company drops below the minimum requirements for listing on the Big Board, it is in danger of being delisted. The Exchange may warn the company and tell it to get its house in order. But if there is no significant improvement after a time, the stock may be removed, or delisted, from the board. This is roughly the equivalent of a one-way ticket to oblivion.

Thus, the second reason for not buying low-priced stocks on the Big Board is that too often they represent a company that is on its way out.

OTHER EXCHANGES

Besides the New York Stock Exchange, there are many other exchanges. The most well known is the American

Stock Exchange. Between 1980 and 1985, the total number of shares traded on the New York Stock Exchange virtually doubled. That of AMEX, however, remained relatively unchanged. As of this writing, AMEX ranks roughly sixth in dollar volume of exchanges worldwide. (NASDAQ, as we'll see, is technically not an auction exchange.)

DOLLAR VOLUME OF EXCHANGES

1. New York Stock Exchange
2. Tokyo Stock Exchange
3. NASDAQ
4. London Stock Exchange
5. Zurich Stock Exchange
6. German Republic Stock Exchange
7. AMEX

AMEX is the little sister of the New York Stock Exchange. Its listing requirements are not as stringent and the average price per share is not as high. However, to my way of thinking, much of what was said about the Big Board applies here as well. It is still not an appropriate arena for low-priced stocks. We are not going to search much on AMEX, either.

In addition, there are numerous smaller regional exchanges, which provide an auction market across the country.

These include the following:

Midwest Stock Exchange
Pacific Coast Stock Exchange
Philadelphia Stock Exchange (PBW)
Cincinnati Stock Exchange
Boston Stock Exchange
Spokane Stock Exchange
Salt Lake City Stock Exchange

Most of these exchanges actually trade stocks that are also listed on the Big Board, although they do encourage regional stocks.

In later chapters we will look at several of these exchanges with regard to low-priced stocks. In addition, we will also pay particular attention to the Vancouver, British Columbia (Canada) Stock Exchange, which is a true penny stock exchange.

WHERE THE PENNIES AREN'T

These, then, are the major *auction* exchanges. However, as we've noted, in most cases a low-priced stock that we might find appealing probably won't be listed here (with certain exceptions).

We've looked at these exchanges not to find out where the pennies are, but instead to get a perspective, to set the stage. We've seen the traditional investment markets for investors.

Now, let's move on to something that may not be quite so traditional (although it certainly has a long history). Let's move on to the markets where the pennies are. In the next chapters we'll discuss the OTC markets and their opportunities.

FINDING THE PENNIES—THE OTC MARKET

When a new investor begins searching for penny stocks, he or she may ask a broker, "I can't find the penny stocks—where's the list?"

Most brokers may try to dissuade the investors from journeying down that "treacherous" path to the pennies. But if the investor is insistent, the broker may dump a telephone-book-size stack of stock lists on his or her lap and say, "You're on your own!"

In other words, the traditional broker (one who day in and day out makes a living trading the Big Board) probably isn't going to be encouraging or helpful with regard to pennies. If you're an investor who wants to get started in the field, therefore, you're going to find that, at least at first, you're pretty much out on your own.

But don't fret. In this chapter we're going to take a look at where we need to go to find the penny stocks.

Most penny stocks can be found on the over-the-counter market. However, unlike the auction exchanges we were looking at in the last chapter, where the action, so to speak, takes place on the floor of a central building, in the OTC market (to paraphrase Gertrude Stein), "There's no there, there."

The OTC market doesn't have an "auction floor" where sales take place. There is no continuous auction going on where brokers for buyers and brokers for sellers compete in a supply/demand situation to determine the price of a stock. A perfect example of this is the Denver market. An enormous amount of OTC oil and gas stock used to be handled in Denver during the days of the oil boom, and a great many penny stocks still change hands there. Yet, there is no official floor for a Denver exchange in the sense that there is one for the New York Stock Exchange. Instead there is the Denver OTC market.

This is a quieter market in a sense. It's conceivable that some time may pass between OTC stock transactions. Depending on the stock and demand for it, it might be hours, days, or even weeks between transactions. Or sales might be hot and heavy for a stock that's in particular demand. Sales take place only when someone wants to buy or sell a particular stock. No buyers or sellers, no market.

While at first glance this might seem like a small market, it is in reality the largest stock market of all. It accounts for *all* those other stocks that aren't listed on the New York Stock Exchange and its relatives. It's the unseen giant where as many as 30,000 different companies in this country alone have their stocks.

A DEALER/TRADER MARKET

The OTC market works because the participants are not only brokers, but are also dealers. The participants don't just act for investors, they also buy and sell stock for their own account.

It's important to see this difference between the OTC market and the auction market. In an auction market, when we want to buy a stock, we call up a broker. She gets hold of her firm's floor person and, acting on our account, tries to buy. This means going to a specialist or another broker who represents someone who wants to sell. When your broker representing you finds another broker representing a seller, a sale is made.

In the OTC market it's a bit different. We call up our broker and want to buy an over-the-counter stock. But remember, there is no exchange floor where brokers representing sellers are waiting to sell. Our broker instead must now locate someone who is willing to sell that stock to us.

Think of how hard it would be for our broker to find an individual investor who happened to want to sell that stock just when we wanted to buy. We might have to wait a very long time for such a person to show up. Without an auction floor, the chances of running into a seller for that stock would be remote.

Were it necessary for our broker to find an individual stock investor who wanted to sell just when we wanted to buy without having an exchange, there would be virtually no market. We wouldn't be able to buy and sellers wouldn't be able to sell stock.

However, do you remember that in the Big Board there were the specialists who dealt in specific stocks and made markets? They acted as a lubricant to keep the market flowing smoothly.

In the OTC market there are dealers who not only are the lubricant, but who virtually are the market itself. These are firms that have agreed to be market makers in particular stocks. They acquire an inventory of the stock themselves and then offer to sell it at any time to anyone who wants to buy. Or offer to buy at any time from anyone who wants to sell. They "deal" in the stock. To carry our analogy to an extreme, this is a market where the grease becomes the motor.

Because there are market makers for specific stocks (frequently more than one market maker per stock), when we tell our broker to buy an OTC stock for us, we've actually given her a fairly easy task.

Our broker now only has to find the market maker who deals in the stock we want. (We'll see how she does this in a moment.) Once she finds out the name of the firm that is making a market in the particular stock we want, she calls up that firm and begins to negotiate.

PRICE IN OTC STOCKS

Because there is no auction where supply and demand are continuously setting the price, in the OTC market, what we'll pay for the stock is a matter of negotiation. Our broker and the dealer negotiate back and forth for a while over the phone (or computer), our broker trying to get the best price for us, the dealer trying to get the best price for the market maker. Eventually a deal is struck and the sale made.

Notice that here our broker dealt with a *dealer*. She dealt with a firm that probably owned the stock we were buying, not with a broker for another investor who was selling. In this case the brokerage house probably was acting as a principal. It was selling *its own stock* to us.

DIFFERENCES BETWEEN AN AUCTION AND A TRADE

There are a number of important differences between an OTC trade and an auction, as we've seen, and we should be aware of them. Here are three:

1. An auction takes place on the floor of an exchange. An OTC trade often takes place over the phone between two brokers, one of whom may be acting as a dealer.
2. In an auction the price is constantly set by the forces of supply and demand on a moment-to-moment basis. In an OTC trade the price is set by negotiation with the market maker/dealer, who presumably is also affected by supply and demand for the stock.
3. In an auction, there is a single price for a stock determined by the auction process. In an OTC trade there is a price "range." The range is the difference between the price the market maker will pay you to buy the stock and the price he asks from you when he sells the stock.

AN INTRODUCTION TO BID/ASK

This price range for OTC stock can be confusing to those new to the field. Since it's critical to low-priced stock investment, however, it's vital that it be thoroughly understood. Let's compare it again with an auction price.

We'll say we want to buy IBM on the Big Board; the price may be $120 a share. We buy 100 shares at $120 apiece (plus commission). A few minutes later we have a change of heart and decide to sell. It just happens that the price hasn't changed, so we sell at $120 (plus commission). We essentially bought and sold at the same price and our only actual costs were the commissions.

In an OTC trade there is no single price. Rather, there is a "bid/ask" range. The "bid" will represent the price at which the market maker will buy the stock from us or any other investor. The "ask" is the price at which he will sell to us or any other investor. For example, the bid may be twenty cents a share, while the ask may be twenty-five cents. If we buy the stock, it costs us twenty-five cents.

But if the next minute we want to sell, we can only sell (to this market maker) for twenty cents, or an immediate loss of a nickel a share for us.

That nickel a share represents the market maker's cost of doing business and a profit. (A commission may be tacked on top of this.)

As should be obvious, an OTC trade is quite different from an auction. It tends to be much more a matter of negotiation, which is another reason why the investor needs to plan investments carefully.

FINDING THE MARKET

We'll return to bid/ask in a few pages to see how it influences our investment strategy, but first let's consider how our broker found that market maker to begin with. (This, after all, is the heart of our interest—where are the penny stocks!)

There are over four thousand registered OTC brokerage companies and many times that number of brokers selling OTC stocks. How did our broker find a firm that was making a market in the one stock we wanted to buy?

The SEC, or Securities and Exchange Commission, oversees all stock trading. However, with regard to OTC stock, it has in effect delegated much of the regulating to the National Association of Securities Dealers (NASD). (NASD membership is an absolute minimum for any broker you are dealing with.)

PINK SHEETS

The NASD oversees trading in about thirty thousand different over-the-counter stocks. (As noted, this is why the

OTC market is considered the largest in the world.) Virtually *all* of these stocks are listed daily in the "pink sheets."

The pink sheets are published by the National Quotation Bureau, Inc. They are indeed pink, are about half a foot wide and nearly two feet long. They come in a stack about as thick as a major city phone book.

The pink sheets are vital to a penny stock buyer because they list the market makers for each stock. If you want to find out what stocks are available and who's making a market in them, you will need to know about the "pinks."

While it is possible to subscribe to the pink sheets, the cost is prohibitive for most investors. It costs $42 a month plus $16 a month for timely delivery. All brokerage houses subscribe, however. Therefore, what you need to do is to make friends with a broker. Since they normally throw out the pink sheets at the end of each day, they should be willing to let you have them. Getting a copy will introduce you to the world of penny stocks.

NASDAQ

Of course, having to check the pinks for market makers, then having to call the makers for their current quotes, is really a rather primitive approach to handling stocks in our modern day. The NASD wrestled with this very problem: how to quickly and efficiently find the market maker and quote for a given stock.

Their solution, begun in 1971, was NASDAQ, which stands for National Association of Securities Dealers Automated Quotations system. This is an enormous computer network that is piped into each of the NASD's member firms.

NASDAQ lists *only the biggest and most active of the*

OTC stocks, about five thousand of them. If we want to find the market maker of a stock listed on NASDAQ, we just go to a member firm's office and have the broker call up the stock on the computer. In an instant we will have on-screen the name of each market maker as well as his or her retail bid/ask for the stock. Not only that, but since most stocks listed by NASDAQ have many market makers (the average is eleven), the computer will show the high bid and the low ask among the market makers.

Today NASDAQ is the third largest stock trading market in the world (after only the New York and Tokyo Stock Exchanges). In dollar volume in 1984 it did roughly seven times the volume of AMEX, the next biggest American trading market. (Remember, of course, that both the Big Board and AMEX are auction markets with a trading floor. NASDAQ doesn't have any "there, there." It exists only on computer screens and over the phone lines of NASD member firms.)

NASDAQ, by bringing computers to the world of OTC stock, revolutionized the industry and created the second largest functioning stock market in the country.

THE KINDS OF COMPANIES ON NASDAQ

NASDAQ, like the Big Board, Amex, and other trading markets, has strict requirements for listing. In general they require that a company have a minimum number of shares, market value, and net worth or net income for the company. *In some cases they also require a minimum bid price of $3.*

When a company is getting started, there are many things it needs, usually including visibility, market share, and investors. Investors not only provide capital, but they also support the company.

One way to get all three of the above and more is to be listed on a major exchange. However, as we've seen, getting listed on the Big Board can be difficult.

Getting listed on NASDAQ, however, is somewhat less difficult. The company doesn't have to be as old and established. And once listed, the company's stock now has a major market in which to trade.

Another way of looking at it is that it's all symbolic, literally. When a company gets listed on NASDAQ, it's given a symbol. This symbol is usually the first few letters of its name. For example, Apple Computers is listed as *Apple C.*

This NASDAQ symbol can mean success or failure to many companies. When a company has a symbol, any NASD broker can punch the symbol into the computer and call up the stock. This means that it can easily be traded. In other words, the NASD symbol is an entrée into the world of investors.

To put it yet another way, few people will buy a product until it gets to market. The NASDAQ symbol is a sort of ticket to the marketplace.

Additionally, because of the requirements for being listed on NASDAQ, many investors are inclined to look with favor on listed companies.

BREAKING INTO PRINT

This all comes to roost in publicity. When we buy a stock, generally we want to be able to follow its course on a regular basis. We want to be able, for example, to look in the paper to see how that stock is doing.

If the stock is with NASDAQ, that's often possible. NASDAQ releases to the media two "recommended" lists, which are then published in major newspapers in this country and even worldwide.

The first list is called the OTC "national list" and is the one most commonly printed. The second list is called the "additional list," which appears in some of the larger papers. These lists give the company symbol, the recent volume, and bid and ask for the stock. Inclusion on the lists is determined on the basis of the size of the company and the volume of shares traded. (If you really want to see how good your local paper is, check to see if it has both lists, one, or neither list. Of course, they are all available in the *Wall Street Journal*.)

While not all NASDAQ companies are listed, many are. If you own a company and you need shareholders to provide capital and support, having your stock symbol listed in the paper as part of a major trading market means that investors are more inclined to trust your company, invest in it, and support it. In other words, it may mean the difference between success and failure.

PINKS VS. NASDAQ

Because NASDAQ is such a powerful influence on the market, a common error those new to stocks make is to think that *all* OTC stocks are listed on NASDAQ—in other words, that the terms NASDAQ and OTC are synonymous. Nothing could be further from the truth.

OTC STANDS FOR *ANY* OVER-THE-COUNTER STOCK (about 30,000 different stocks in this country alone.)

NASDAQ STANDS FOR WHAT ARE USUALLY THE *TOP* OTC STOCKS (about 5,000 of them).

That means that there are twenty-five thousand OTC

stocks that are *not* listed on NASDAQ (but which can provide excellent buying opportunities for the penny stock investor). These stocks have *no* NASDAQ symbol and never appear on the NASDAQ lists.

Another difference between a NASDAQ listing and an OTC pink sheet listing is that typically the NASDAQ listing in a newspaper will show the stock's symbol, its volume (if available), it's week's high and low bid, and the change from the previous week. On the other hand, a non-NASDAQ stock listed on the pinks will often just show its market maker(s). To find a quote, you'll have to call the market maker.

WHAT TO DO ONCE YOU'VE LOCATED THE PENNIES

In this chapter we've covered the basics of the OTC market. We've seen where the pennies are listed and we've delved into the differences between the NASDAQ list and the pinks.

But once we've gotten hold of the pinks and the NASDAQ list, what do we do next? How do we determine which stocks to buy?

There are at least three more steps we need to take, and they all can be done simultaneously:

1. Check with investment advisories that give information about penny stocks.
2. Find out how the market really works and get a winning strategy.
3. Locate a good broker.

In the next chapter we'll begin by looking at the investment advisories.

INVESTMENT ADVISORIES

■

If you've read through this book thus far, I'm sure you've come to realize that in penny stocks, knowledge is vital. The problem, of course, is that accurate information in the field tends to be difficult to come by.

Because we are dealing with small companies, the regular news channels don't maintain very good coverage. In addition, sometimes the companies as well as the underwriters will "leak" information that may exaggerate the potential of a company. Finally, there is always the temptation on the part of those reporting to themselves invest in a company and then promote its stock through carefully placed "news" items.

For the investor, particularly one new to the field, finding accurate information, therefore, can be a real problem. It's hard to know where to start looking.

Well, this is the place to start in terms of getting informed. In this chapter I've listed many of the different investment advisories and news publications. I've also put down my own comments regarding them. Even if you're not ready to start investing, subscribing to one or more is an excellent way to become familiar with the market.

NOTE: I am neither recommending nor endorsing any of these publications. While most endeavor to provide accurate news information, the author specifically disclaims any liability for loss caused by relying on any information or recommendations contained in any of these publications.

(Also note that costs quoted may be different by the time you read this information.)

The National OTC Stock Journal
Weekly (Under $80 per year)
1780 S. Bellaire St., Suite 400
Denver, CO 80222

This is one of the most widely read journals in penny stocks. Although it states it covers stocks "under ten dollars," it's coverage of what's happening in pennies has been both comprehensive and credible. For anyone who wants to invest in pennies, this is a "must."

COVERAGE: News Affecting Low-Priced Stocks
People in the News
NASDAQ Volume Leaders
Columns:
- Press Releases
- Market Talk
- Editorial Opinion
- Corporate Comments
- Corporate Reports
- Spotlight (featuring newsletters)

Pulse of the Market
(featuring multiple indices)

New Issue Summaries
Quotes (OTC market)
New Issue Aftermarket Quotes
New Issues in Registration
Rule 144 (insider) Proposed Stock Sales
Paid Advertising

PennyStock News
Weekly ($50 per year)
8930 J Oakland Center
Columbia, MD 21045

This is a highly readable tabloid, which contains information on the penny stock field. It contains many columns of special interest. However, it was the subject of an SEC investigation in 1984 involving alleged improprieties.

COVERAGE: News Affecting Penny Stocks
PSN Index
Volume Watch
Company Profiles
New Issues Update
Market Digest
Insider Trading
New Issues Ratings
New Issues in Registration
New Issues Market Performance
Updates
PSB Recommendations
Quotations (OTC)
Warrant Watch
Columns:
- Investor Notebook
- Ahead of the Pack

People in Business
New Issues Update
Corporate Corner
Paid Advertising

Penny Stock Preview and *Low-Priced Stock Digest*
Monthly (*Preview*—$48, *Digest*—$68 per year)
Idea Publishing Corporation
55 East Afton Ave.
Yardley, PA 19067

The *Low-Priced Stock Digest* is a newsletter that is a summary of other newsletters. The editor claims to read more than a hundred other newsletters a month and then pick the best of what's been said for this publication. I have found it to be extremely informative.

The *Penny Stock Preview* is a newsletter that features new issues. It gives brief descriptions of new stocks and has a "Sneak Preview" section, which gives stocks, underwriters, and prices of recent issues. Also helpful are an "Underwriter's Box Score," in which it rates the success of underwriters in bringing new issues to market, and "Top 10 Percentage Gainers," in which it rates the best new issues of the past year.

The Cheap Investor
Published by Bill Mathews
Monthly ($78 per year)
36 King Arthur Court
Suite 10
Northlake, IL 60164

This is a newsletter that makes buy and sell recommendations. It specializes in stocks under ten dollars. It also features a "Blue Cheap Index" on its favored stocks. It includes analyses of companies and explanations of why they may do better or worse in the future.

The Prospector
Published by The Penny Mining Prospector, Inc.,
Darrell Brookstein
1096 "D" Coast Village Rd.
Santa Barbara, CA 93108

This newsletter "prospects" for good mining stocks. The publisher makes no bones about stating up front that he is a "registered representative and major shareholder of First Georgetown Securities, Inc. . . ." which is "the only stockbroker he recommends for the execution of trades."

The newsletter contains its own index of penny mining stocks as well as buy and sell recommendations.

Uptrend
Published by Continental, Carlisle, Douglas; editor: Henry Huber
Published every three weeks ($55 for six issues, $220 for twenty-four issues)
Investment Services, Ltd.
P.O. Box 49333
Four Bentall Centre
Vancouver, B. S. V7X 1L4

This is a Canadian stock newsletter. The editor analyzes a great many stocks and provides a rating system for grading them. He also provides information about trading in the Vancouver market. If you're interested in Vancouver, then this is a "must" newsletter.

The Silver Baron
Edited by Elliott Pearson
About every three weeks ($125 per year)
350 S. Center St.
Reno, NV 89501

This newsletter tries to predict those inexpensive mining stocks that are likely to do well in the future. It maintains updates on previous recommendations as well as conducting in-depth analyses of current recommendations.

WHERE TO FIND OUT ABOUT OTHER NEWSLETTERS

The *OTC Stock Journal* publishes a "Special Report," which lists some of the publications noted above as well as a great many others. This report sells for ten dollars. (Write directly to the *OTC Stock Journal* at the address noted previously.)

WAYS TO WIN IN PENNIES

In one sense penny stocks are an easy investment to figure out. There are really only three ways to win. (There are countless ways to lose, but that's the subject of a later chapter.) These three ways can quickly be listed:

1. Go for long-term growth.
2. Play a stock.
3. Buy new issues.

Of course, if you're new to penny stocks, just having this list isn't going to be all that helpful. You have to know what the three methods mean and how to use them successfully. That's what we'll get started on in this chapter.

NOTE: Before starting this chapter, it's important to understand that it is only part of a whole. Here we're going to look at how to win. In a later chapter we're going to look at how to avoid losing. *Don't just read this chapter and think you've got it all. Be sure to at least read Chapter 10, "Pitfalls in Pennies," as well.*

THE SEARCH FOR LOW-PRICED GROWTH STOCKS

In our search for low-priced stocks in which we might invest, we have covered three tiers. The first tier was represented by the Big Board, AMEX, and similar exchanges. I noted that it was unlikely we would find stocks there that would be appealing because in many cases, those that had a low enough price were from companies on their way down-and-out.

The second tier is the NASDAQ stocks. Are we likely to find good low-priced stocks here?

The answer is yes. In my opinion one of the best places to find low-priced *growth* stocks is on NASDAQ. (Although we shouldn't be under the illusion that NASDAQ is filled with stocks under five dollars. Even here they are the exception, rather than the rule.)

WHAT IS A GROWTH STOCK?

Since the first category for winning with pennies is to buy growth stocks, let's take a few paragraphs to define them. We'll use the old tried-and-true Wall Street definition here. A growth stock is one in which the earnings of the company are plowed back into the company so that it grows bigger and bigger and becomes worth more and more.

Companies that have made it to NASDAQ have often overcome that first hurdle that weeds out the weak, the unlikely to succeed, the "no-chance" companies. They have survived their first years and have shown they can make an income (not necessarily a profit, but an income).

Some of these companies are going to be the IBMs and the Xeroxes and even the General Motors of tomorrow. Unlike the Big Board, where a low price for a stock often indicates trouble, on NASDAQ a low price may indicate a fledgling company just getting off the ground.

It all becomes a matter of direction. Think of low price on the Big Board with an arrow pointed downward. Think of low price on NASDAQ with an arrow pointed upward. (Unfortunately, sometimes the arrow goes the other way for NASDAQ companies as well.)

Of course, this certainly is not true for all NASDAQ stocks. It may not even be true for most of them. But if we can identify those stocks that indeed represent companies that are growing, and indeed have the arrow pointed upward, we are going to be successful.

Find a good growth stock, stick with it, and we can grow rich beyond our wildest dreams. Their growth can become our growth. We can watch them move from a few dollars a share to ultimately hundreds of dollars. It's the old story of hitching our wagon to a shooting star. If we pick a star among the NASDAQ stocks, we, too, can shoot across the sky.

Of course, the eternal question is, "Which stock?" We'll have much more to say about picking winners from the national list later. Suffice it to say here that the first place we are likely to find winning stocks is the second tier of stock investment—those stocks that have NASDAQ symbols.

THE SEARCH FOR PLAYING STOCKS

I define a stock for "playing" as one in which we really don't worry about growth. For a variety of reasons (explained in a later chapter) we think the stock is going to make a big jump. We want to get in quick and then get out quick. Where are we likely to find stocks for playing?

The answer is the third tier, the pink sheets. We are going to find thousands of start-up companies on the pink sheets, some of which will blossom in just a few weeks. If we're careful, do our homework, and have a pinch of luck, we'll be able to do very well playing winners from the pinks.

We'll discuss how to play a stock in great detail in Chapter 8. For now, however, let's just remember that it's the second way to win.

BUYING NEW ISSUES

The final way of making a profit in penny stocks that we'll discuss is to buy new issues.

A new issue is new stock issued by a company. It could be a company already in business that already has public stock and is now coming out with more of it. Such a company could be on the Big Board, or AMEX, or on NASDAQ.

But what we are more likely to be concerned with is a company that's been private and is just now going public. This is its first public offering. This is the kind of new issue that penny stock investors scramble to get.

Why?

Because when the penny stock market is hot, there is no place where money can be made faster than in new issues. Everybody wants them; investors don't even care what the company is, who manages it, what its product may be. If it's a new issue, *Buy!*

Of course, such investing is foolhardy, and the old saying about a fool and his money soon being parted certainly holds true here. We'll devote an entire chapter (Chapter 9) to the ins and outs of new issues. But for now, let's just see where and why the money is made here.

THE STORY BEHIND NEW ISSUES

BESTNEWPRODUCT company consists of six engineers. At one time they all worked for a major computer firm. But they got laid off in the computer downturn of 1984-85. So they decided to go to work for themselves. Opening up a "laboratory" in one of their garages, they have invented a computer that talks to the user.

They feel it's a remarkable invention. Instead of a keyboard, when you want to write a letter, you simply dictate it. The computer understands the words and produces a written page, every sentence in correct context, every word properly spelled.

Now they want to produce the product. . . . Only, that takes money. They decide to raise the money by going public. They already have a corporation. Now the corporation will issue stock.

The first thing they do is get a brokerage house to handle the sale, or "underwrite" it. Typically, an underwriter is the same company we were just introduced to as a market maker. As an underwriter, the brokerage company helps get the stock to market. Once it's on the market (called the "after market"), they handle it as the market maker.

The issue comes out at twenty cents a share. There are going to be five million shares, which if sold out will raise $1 million. The company will get $750,000 of this, paying the underwriter $250,000 for its efforts. (In a new issue the company pays the commission, not you, the buyer.)

A SUCCESS STORY

However, as soon as investors hear what the company has to offer, they go wild. A talking computer! It's sensational. The five million shares are gobbled up, with plenty of people waiting.

The stock is issued at twenty cents a share. Because there's so much demand for the company, it quickly rises. Within weeks it's at fifty cents a share.

Let's pause in our description of the company to note the position of the investor who bought the new issue. If he or she was lucky enough to get it at the twenty-cent price before it hit after market, this investor has made a neat profit of thirty cents *on each share*. The investor now can decide to keep the stock hoping for a much higher return, or sell.

In this case, our investor decides to sell. Which turns out to be a wise move. A short time later the BESTNEW-PRODUCT company comes out with it's first product. Oh, the computer talks, all right, but it only speaks in guttural Hindustani. The market for it is severely limited and the stock price plunges to one cent a share. A few months later the company disappears from view.

A QUICK RIDE

Does this really happen? Yes, all the time. New companies filled with promise are continually coming out. A few do indeed have products that become successful. But the vast majority, whether in pharmaceuticals, high tech, mining, or whatever, will fail.

Nevertheless, for a few breathless weeks or months they may ride high, and it is on this *anticipation* that investors buy. You see, many investors in new issues *don't really care* if the company is going to ultimately succeed or not. As long as it has "sizzle," as long as it has "sex appeal," they'll buy the stock hoping that the public will clamber aboard. Then these shrewd investors will bail out before the crash.

Of course, it doesn't always happen that way. Many times new issues won't go up in price, but will instead go straight down. Other times the company will have a truly revolutionary product and the stock will seem to never stop climbing, causing those "shrewd" investors who sold early to pull out their hairs.

Nevertheless, the new issues market is a place where profits—very quick profits—are made in penny stocks. Of course, there are substantial pitfalls, as we'll see. However, for the person who wants to become an investor in pennies, new issues is an arena that cannot be ignored.

THE MECHANICS OF BUYING AND SELLING PENNY (OTC) STOCKS

We briefly summarized the three ways to win at penny stocks. We'll devote the next three chapters to covering each in detail. But now, let's get down to brass tacks with the market. Let's see how it really operates.

When we buy a penny stock, the transaction is handled much the same as it is for any other OTC stock. We talk to our broker and decide to make a purchase. The broker fills out a ticket and takes it to the trading desk.

This desk is occupied by a person who specializes in locating the market maker and handling the transaction. The trader locates the stock we want, haggles trying to get the best price, and finally a sale is made. We are told we have the stock and the price we paid. Eventually we receive a confirmation slip (called a "confirm" in the trade), which indeed confirms what we already know.

COMMISSIONS

When we play a stock, that is, buy it in the anticipation of selling after it goes up quickly, we need to buy as low as possible. After all, this is strictly a matter of buying low and selling high. If we do it the other way around, the results will not in the least please us.

With true penny stocks, those in the under-a-dollar range, the commission can become a significant factor. It can, in fact, be the difference between making a profit or losing money. Therefore, if we're going to play with stocks, it's vital that we understand how the commission structure works.

The amount of the commission can vary enormously. This is something to straighten out with your broker before you buy. It is worth noting that there is no "set" or "required" fee schedule. The National Association of Securities Dealers requires that its members charge fees that are both fair and reasonable. However, the interpretation of "reasonable and fair" can vary quite a bit, depending on your perspective. In addition, some brokers have a "minimum fee" regardless of the amount of the transaction. If the minimum fee happens to be $35 and your total stock cost is $100, then the fee is close to 35 percent of the cost of the transaction!

Note: The reason for the minimum fee is that many brokerage houses use an accounting system that allocates a percentage of overhead to every transaction. Thus, regardless of the amount of the transaction, the house's accounting system may determine that there is an automatic expense of between $20 and $30 involved. Hence, we have the minimum fee. (The minimum fee may not even make a profit for the house!)

LOCATING THE FEE

In addition to the amount of the fee, there is also the problem of determining what it actually was. This can be a bit more difficult than it first seems.

If the broker we deal with goes to a market maker to find the stock for us, then his commission should dutifully be noted on the confirm slip. We'll see just what he charged.

On the other hand, if we buy directly from the market maker (as some brokers advise), then we probably won't see a commission tacked onto the confirm. That doesn't, of course, mean that no commission was charged. It just means that the commission was added into the spread.

BUYING DIRECT FROM THE MARKET MAKER

You'll recall that with OTC stock there is a spread between the bid price and the ask price. For example, a market maker could have a bid of fifteen cents and an ask of twenty cents. Bid fifteen/ask twenty (or fifteen at twenty as it is sometimes called) means that if you want to buy, you must pay twenty cents. If you want to sell, you will get fifteen cents.

This is generally referred to as the "retail" price or the "advertised" price. When our broker calls up, however, he negotiates a price. Perhaps instead of twenty, he determines that the market maker is desperate to sell and so gets us a price of eighteen cents. When we get our confirm, we see a price of eighteen cents plus whatever the broker's commission happened to be.

On the other hand, let's say we go directly to the market maker. We are probably going to end up paying the retail price. In this case, it might be twenty or twenty-one cents. (The price might have mysteriously gone up a cent or two just before our order came in.)

When we get back our confirm from the market maker, it would show only that we had paid, for example, twenty-one cents a share for the stock. There would be no commission.

However, we did, in effect, pay a commission. The stock was just "marked up" (its price increased) to account for it. If the price turned out to be twenty-one cents, well then, the commission was just that much higher. The point is that the piper must be paid. There is a commission one way or the other. This is the reason some other brokers suggest you *never* buy direct from a market maker.

Note: in some cases the broker we go to will handle the sale directly as a principal. In other words, the broker's firm may have the stock on hand in its own account. It will then sell it to us. This is essentially the same as buying from a market maker. The confirm may not show a commission, but you can be sure it's there in a markup on the stock.

MARKDOWNS ON SELLING

This commission process works in a similar way when it's time to sell. If we go through a broker who then buys from a market maker, we may get a slightly better than retail bid price plus a commission tacked on.

On the other hand, if we're dealing directly with the market maker or with a broker/principal, we may find that the bid price is *lower* than we anticipated. The stock was "marked down" (we got less for our stock than we anticipated). The lower price paid to us means that the spread was increased. This, in effect, amounts to a tacked-on commission.

CALCULATING OUR COSTS

What's important here is not to get alarmed by either the size of the commission (unless it's unreasonable—we'll have more to say about that later) or the method of it's being assessed. We must understand that the commission is part of doing business in penny stocks. It's a volatile, sometimes thin market. The market makers and the brokers have to make their share in order to stay in business. After all, without them, there wouldn't be any penny market at all.

The point is that if we are going to play a stock, to win, we have to win fairly big. For example, if the spread is indeed five cents, as it was in our preceding example, then the stock is going to have to go up five cents in price *before* we break even. It's going to have to go a lot higher for us to make a profit.

Of course, many do, and that's why people play the field. In a field as highly speculative as this, however, more stocks don't succeed than do. For example, the stock we bought at twenty cents may dip down to an ask of ten cents. Even though the stock has only gone down five cents in price, if we sell, we will lose half our investment (bought at twenty cents, sold at ten cents) because of the spread.

All of which leads us to the first rule of playing a stock. You have to hit a winner to succeed. Just buying and selling stocks, even if they don't move in price, will eventually use up all your investment money.

Some people start with $500 and either aren't careful or aren't lucky, and don't hit a winner. It's easy to see how very soon they end up with nothing. If they are new to the field, they may begin thinking they were cheated or that the broker churned their funds. ("Churned" means buying and selling stocks in our account simply to generate commissions for the broker.)

While both those possibilities could have occurred, more likely they simply lost their money to the spread. They just didn't realize that without hitting a winner, they would quickly use up their capital and be out of the market.

But that's just the way it is when you play the pennies. You're risking your money on hitting it big. If you're going to worry about losing your investment, then you don't belong here.

WINNING AT PENNIES

As I noted at the beginning of this chapter, the three ways of winning at pennies are not hard to define. They are:

1. Buy for growth.
2. Play a stock.
3. Buy new issues.

To these we should also add at least two commonsense rules that we've touched on in various places. They are:

DON'T BUY JUST ONE STOCK: We should try to get at least four or five stocks rather than just one. In most cases this increases our chances of hitting at least one winner. And in this field, one winner can quickly offset half a dozen losers.

START WITH A MINIMUM INVESTMENT: We should come in with a minimum investment, say $500. We should be able to invest this money and not fear that the world will end if we lose it.

To win at pennies, you have to know how to play the game. In this chapter we've outlined the game as it stands. We've briefly looked at the mechanics—in a sense, we've been given the basic rules of play. In the next chapters we'll delve deeper and look at some of the winning "tricks of the trade" to see where the money is to be made.

PICKING GROWTH STOCKS

I recently had occasion to talk with two unrelated people who invested in low-priced stocks, one successfully and the other with little success. One had spent a great deal of time carefully analyzing the market and several dozen stocks. The other had literally taken a long list of stocks, pinned it to a wall, and thrown a felt-tip pen at it. (He couldn't find a dart, so he used the next best thing.)

Which one of these two investors do you think was the successful one, and which was not?

Interestingly enough, the one who threw the pen had picked a stock that had nearly tripled in value! The other investor had picked three stocks to buy. One had gone down drastically in price while the other two had shown little to no movement.

Does this mean, therefore, that throwing darts (or pens) at a list of stocks is the way to pick winners?

NO ANALYSIS IS PERFECT

Well, the method certainly does have its advocates, and the preceding example does go to show the fallibility of analysis. There's no doubt that you can spend a lot of time investigating stocks only to come up dry. I know of one individual who spent at least two years carefully analyzing the market only to come up with loser after loser. (He subsequently picked a number of winners and walked off with $150,000 in profit.)

Nevertheless, I don't pick stocks by the dart/pen method and I suspect you won't want to, either. Most of us would prefer an educated guess to a wild guess. And that's what analyzing the market to pick winners actually comes down to—educated guessing.

KNOW WHAT YOU'RE LOOKING FOR

The first step in making an educated guess is to narrow the field. What are you looking for in a stock? From the last chapter we should recall that there are at least three ways to win:

1. Buy a stock for growth.
2. Play a stock.
3. Buy new issues.

One might think that the way to begin is to examine the market and then see which of the three methods offers the most immediate opportunity. That, however, is actually a dead-end course. At any given time there's plenty of opportunity available in all three areas.

Rather, the way to proceed is to pick one of the three and then try to find the best stock to fit that category. In this chapter we'll consider the first, buying a stock for growth. In the next chapters we'll look at what's involved in playing a stock and new issues.

FUNDAMENTAL VS. TECHNICAL ANALYSIS

What all stock analysis comes down to are two perspectives—fundamental and technical. A fundamental analysis looks at causes. What might cause a stock to go up (or down) in price? It considers such things as the economy, the health of the company, its earnings, and a host of other indicators.

A technical analysis, on the other hand, is quite different. It looks for patterns in the market. Technical analysts are heavily into charts and use such terms as "rising bottoms" or "falling tops," referring to the sawtooth pattern a stock's price makes on those charts. The underlying goal of a true technician is to identify the pattern (trend) of a stock in the past and project that into the future.

Both fundamental and technical analyses have their advocates. In penny stocks, however, there are some who say that there is no room for technical analysis. Dr. Bob Kirk, a long-time investor and broker, points out that "technical analysis on penny stocks has no basis. Technical analysis assumes the market has equal access to information on the company and this is discounted. With pennies, timely and accurate information is difficult to obtain and verify."

Lest we proceed further without you, the reader, understanding my bias, let me say that I'm a dyed-in-the-wool fundamentalist. I personally believe the way to find winners is through careful analysis of the items likely to cause a stock to move and that technical analysis is just so much hokum.

On the other hand, that does not mean that I would dare to ignore technical analysis. As we'll see shortly, it can be useful in selecting winners when we're playing stocks, but not for the reasons technicians give. For now, on to the fundamentals.

FUNDAMENTALS AND GROWTH STOCK

When we're looking for a growth stock, we're looking for a company whose earnings will multiply and whose stock price will steadily go up. In that case what we are really talking about is long term. We don't buy such a stock today to sell it tomorrow. We buy it to hang on to for years.

When we're buying a stock for long-term growth, we can tend to ignore the moment-to-moment fluctuations of the market. True, we will want to buy on a dip. But dips and small rises tend to even out over time, and if we're in for the long haul, it's more important that we pay attention to the potential for steady growth.

The ideal kind of analysis to use to find this kind of a stock is the fundamental approach. If we discover the reasons that a stock should go up, and if our analysis is correct, then eventually, in spite of passing fads and market ups and downs, that stock should appreciate in price.

Of course, such analysis requires a bit of a track record. A company that's brand new with no track record leaves us little to go on. Therefore, we're going to pick established companies, those that have been around for a while, at least eighteen months at a minimum. And we will probably be searching principally for those companies that have a NASDAQ symbol. That doesn't mean we will automatically eliminate others. It's just that NASDAQ will probably be our basic hunting grounds. (Remember, we're just looking for a *growth* stock here. When we begin looking for a stock to play, we'll have different rules.)

GETTING STARTED

So, how do we get started?

Ideally we will have a list of stocks to consider. Once we have that list, we will take the time to analyze each from a fundamental perspective.

Here are seven different ways to analyze a stock from a fundamental perspective. Look through these seven tests and then, the next time you want to buy a growth stock, apply each of them. If the stock passes all or most of them, it has to be considered a potential winner.

1. Is There Strong Earnings Potential?

Earnings are what a company makes for it's efforts in business. And every investor with any smarts at all looks first at earnings.

This is true in any business. Let's say we're going to buy a racehorse. We have a choice between "Old Blue" and "In The Money." Old Blue has a nice disposition, but during the past year she hasn't won a race and has come in second only twice. She has earned only $7,500. In The Money, on the other hand, has won three of her last five races. Her earnings have come to $80,000.

Now, which horse would you buy?

Obviously, in the harsh business world, a nice disposition holds no candle to hard cash. Old Blue is out and In The Money is going to be our pick.

But why? Just because In The Money had higher earnings than Old Blue in the past doesn't mean it's going to continue in the future.

No, of course it doesn't. In The Money could break a leg tomorrow. But past performance still is one of the best indications of future performance. If In The Money earned $80,000 last year, maybe she'll earn $100,000 this year.

The same reasoning applies to companies. Investors look at past earnings to give them some idea of future earnings. The better past earnings were, the more likely they are to want to buy the company's stock. Many penny stock companies, however, have a history of little to no past earnings.

Investors buy the future

It's important to see, therefore, that investors don't buy *past* earnings. They buy *future* earnings.

In other words, if a company called "HitItBig" has strong earnings, investors will buy because they hope for even stronger earnings in the future. It's those future earnings they are looking at when they buy. The past earnings are the indicator, but future earnings are the motivator.

Beware of dividends

Earnings are not dividends. Dividends are what a company pays to stockholders. They come out of earnings. If a company earns a dollar a share, it can decide to pay that whole dollar to its stockholders. Or it can decide to pay only fifty cents. Or it can opt to pay nothing.

Smart investors look for companies with earnings and little to no dividends. The reason is that when earnings aren't paid out, they are plowed back into the company.

Money reinvested in the company means even higher earnings in the future. It means stronger growth.

Of course, one must be careful, particularly with smaller companies. Earnings plowed back into research and development that proves futile, or other nonproductive schemes, aren't going to eventually translate into profits.

2. Does the Stock Have a Low P/E Ratio?

This is the big indicator that most stock analysts always are on the watch for. Many investors feel this indicates whether or not the stock is ripe for buying or is overpriced.

Of course, the problem with many penny stocks is that many have no earnings history at all. We cover that possibility in a few paragraphs. But first, let's consider the company with both price *and* earnings.

The "price per earnings" (P/E) ratio is quite easy to calculate. We simply need to know the earnings per share of a company's stock and it's price per share. (To find the earnings per share—if you know the total earnings, simply divide by the number of shares.)

To find the P/E ratio, divide the earnings into the price (remember, the denominator goes into the numerator). This gives us a ratio. For example, if the stock is selling for $4 a share and the earnings are fifty cents a share, we end up with a ratio of eight:

$$\$4.00 \div .50 = 8$$

Now, for a test of what we know. Suppose we have three stocks and their P/Es are four, eight, and twelve. *Without knowing anything else,* which stock is the best buy?

Without knowing anything else, we would have to go for the first stock, stock A in the following table. To see why, suppose that each stock has the same earnings, fifty cents. Here's what they would cost to buy.

STOCK A	STOCK B	STOCK C
Earnings $ .50	$ .50	$ .50
Ratio 4	8	12
Price $2.00	$4.00	$6.00

Since each stock has the same earnings, the one that costs us the least to buy (stock A) is obviously the best deal.

The problem with a low P/E ratio

I have seen brokers advise clients to look *only* for those low-priced stocks with low P/Es for just the reasons cited above. Frequently the advice takes the form of, "Only buy stocks with ratios below eight (or below ten or whatever)." This advice is simpleminded in the extreme.

Remember, our example had as its constraint, "without knowing anything else." In reality, we always know something else, often quite a bit more.

Maybe stock C's ratio is so high because it's growing superfast and everyone wants to get it. Perhaps it's a company that's come out with a proven cancer test that's currently being marketed in Europe. Investors feel that within a few years, when it finally gets FDA approval for sales here in the United States, that fifty-cent dividend might be $2 or $3. Hence the high ratio.

On the other hand, maybe stock A has such a low ratio because people feel the company is stagnant. It's earned that same fifty cents a share for the past three years and it's not going anywhere. (The company makes clothes hangers and it's not going to improve its market share or its earnings.) Stock A might simply be a no-growth company.

It's for this reason that the much vaunted P/E ratio has to be taken with a grain of salt . . . and with a lot of other investigating. It's a great indicator, but it should not be the *only* indicator you use.

(NOTE: The price per share of a stock is given in any newspaper that lists that stock. The earnings per share shows up in a variety of places, such as the *Wall Street Journal*, *Barrons*, or any of the stock rating services such as Standard & Poor. Or you can always ask your broker, who should be able to provide the information.)

When there are no earnings

Some penny stocks have a history of no earnings at all, ever. Yet, the stock is priced at a certain level, say fifty cents a share. With no earnings history at all, how is that price level determined?

It's a good question. I see two possible answers. The first is that the buyers see some potential down the road and the stock's price reflects that enthusiasm. The second is that there really is no justification for the price and that it is being artificially held up (see Chapter 10, "Pitfalls in Pennies").

3. Is the Stock in a Growth Industry?

The next fundamental is an industry analysis. The simple truth is that some industries are better than others. And those that are better change.

Consider computers. Back in the early 1980s, the computer industry was the darling of stock investors. When Apple stock came out, people swarmed to it. It was a good time to buy computer stock . . . of almost any company.

However, sometime during 1984 the public decided that, unlike a can opener and a TV, there might not be a place in every house for a computer (at least not until somebody found out what the average homemaker could do with it). Hence, an industry that had been a "golden boy" suddenly turned sour. When KayPro went public about this time and tried to sell its stock, it encountered difficulty.

The same holds true for all the small-computer-related companies. When the industry as a whole was booming, so, too, were their stocks, *even the stocks of the "also-rans" and "never-will-bes."* On the other hand, once the word got out that the industry was "in a slump," even the substantial computer companies (including IBM for a time) found their stocks depressed.

When you're looking for a low-priced growth stock, keep abreast of what's happening in various industries. Find out which ones are showing overall strong earnings and go there. But be careful that the shine they exhibit today isn't going to tarnish tomorrow.

Look at market share

To those "in the know," this is possibly the single most important indicator of a company's potential. What share of the market does the company now have and what is its potential?

A classic success story here has to be Xerox. When it started out, it had a copier. But it was virtually the only company with a copier that operated well. Consequently, it had almost all of the market.

McDonald's is another. When it started, it was selling hamburgers for fifteen cents apiece. (I know, I bought some of them!) It had virtually the whole low-end fast-food hamburger market to itself. And as the market grew, it grew with it, maintaining a strong market share.

What new company today is in a similar position? Perhaps it's making a new kind of dog leash that won't tangle in the feet of the person walking the dog. It's a small company and its product is just getting to market. But it's got 100 percent of that market because nobody else is making that kind of leash. As pet owners realize the advantage of this product, and as it becomes an accepted household name, it has an excellent chance of maintaining its dominance over that market.

The drawback comes from competition. Could a large Fortune 500 company suddenly move into the field, reposition the product, and take over the market? Does the management have the skill and wits to anticipate and counter such a move?

Can you relate to the product?

This is the personal test. You find a low-priced stock of a company that's manufacturing soundproof earmuffs. It's marketed them in the Northeast so far with good results. It's got virtually the entire market for this kind of product. It's about to move its operation into the West and South. All the earnings tests indicate "go."

But you live in Los Angeles and you say to yourself, "Soundproof earmuffs? They've got to be kidding! Who on earth would buy such a ridiculous thing?"

Do you ignore your own instincts and buy the stock? Or do you reconsider?

I'd trust my instincts. Certainly, I could be wrong. But I figure I'm an average person with average likes and dislikes. If I don't like the product, there are a lot of other people who won't like it, either. There are so many stocks and so many companies out there to choose from that at the very least I should like the product my company manufactures.

4. Is the Stock's Price Low Enough?

We are, after all, looking for low-priced stock. Is this stock that we are considering low enough in price for us?

This is first a personal consideration. Yes, perhaps we'll consider any stock under $5. But what we really want is any stock under fifty cents. We may have found what appears to be the perfect stock from the viewpoint of earnings and market at $3.50 a share, but something is holding us back. Could it be that the price is just not appealing to us?

How does the current price relate to previous prices?

This is the nonpersonal part of our analysis. The stock is selling today for a bid of forty-four cents, ask fifty cents. If that's all we know, then we should *not* buy. In order to buy, we need to know much more.

How much was the stock selling for yesterday, a week ago, a month ago, six months ago, a year ago, eighteen months ago, and two years ago? We need to know the answers to all of these questions before we buy.

It may turn out that two years ago this stock was selling for bid $1.80, ask $2. It's steadily progressed downward until today. If you have this information, would you now buy this stock? (While at first glance the answer is undoubtedly no, it might turn out that the stock was oversold or undervalued at the higher amount and now the price is realistic—it takes investigation.)

On the other hand, maybe the stock started at two cents and has moved steadily upward until it's near fifty cents today. Now would you feel better about buying it? (Maybe you shouldn't. A stock with this kind of a surge may indicate price manipulation—see Chapter 10, on pitfalls.)

Or in yet another case, over the past two years it's had a fifty-two-week high bid of $2 and a fifty-two-week low bid of two cents, and it's been bouncing around in between for the past six months. That paints yet a different picture.

The past performance with regard to highs and lows for the past year should be readily available in your local paper, if the stock is listed. More detailed information on price history should be available from your broker. If worst comes to worst and you want to buy but can't find out this price background, call the company. Somebody there surely knows and can tell you.

What is the book value relative to price?

This is for those who like to see what they are getting. Book value relates to a company's tangible assets. (It's also sometimes called liquidation value.) It's found by going through the balance sheet and performing the following calculations:

START WITH	All tangible assets
DEDUCT	All debts
DEDUCT	*All liabilities*
THE RESULT IS	Liquidation value
DIVIDED BY	*Number of shares*
EQUALS	Book value

The book value, in essence, is what each share of stock would be worth if the company were to be sold and the resulting money given to the shareholders.

If the market price (what the stock is selling for on the market) is *higher* than the book value, the stock is in an overpriced position *at the current time*. If the market price is *lower* than the book value, the stock is in an underpriced position *at the current time*. If both prices are about the same, then the stock is currently priced about right.

At first glance this may seem like a foolproof way to determine what a stock should be selling for. However, remember, investors buy on anticipation of future earnings (and stock values). This book value figure only tells what the stock should be worth today. If its market value is considerably higher, that doesn't mean it's necessarily a bad buy. It may only mean that investors see this as a strong growth stock and are buying in anticipation of future earnings.

Book value is a useful tool only when used in conjunction with what we've already said about earnings. For example, if earnings have been steadily increasing, and other signs are go, *and* the stock's market price is still below book value, then this may be a great opportunity. On the other hand, if earnings are increasing but the stock is way over book price, it may indicate an inflated value, setting the stock up for a potential price drop in the not-too-distant future.

5. Is the Company Healthy?

In an individual, health is sometimes defined as a lack of illness. If we aren't sick with some disease, then we're healthy. This can also be a useful way of assessing the health of a company.

If we're looking to buy the low-priced stock of a company for growth, we want to be sure that the company doesn't have some illness that will cause it to flounder, or worse, to fail. It's important to realize that some companies, like people, can give the impression of health, all the while concealing a serious problem.

With companies there are usually three illnesses that we want to particularly watch out for. They are "overindebtedness," "liabilitiespressure," and "managementitis." Let's consider them one at a time.

Overindebtedness

This is perhaps the most serious problem that can afflict a company in times of high interest rates. Many companies borrow to buy materials for products, to advertise their lines, to meet current obligations. There is nothing wrong with borrowing . . . as long as the company can afford it. When a company can't afford the borrowing, then the creditors come pounding on the doors and sometimes bankruptcy is not far off.

How do we know if a company is borrowing too much? One way is to check the most recent income statement. Information on larger companies can also be found in "Moody's Investor's Fact Sheets" and the "Stock Reports" issued by Standard & Poor.

The thing to look for is long-term debt. How big is it in relationship to the size of the company?

One way to judge is to divide long-term debt into the equity of the shareholders. (We find shareholders' equity by multiplying book value—described above—by the total number of shares.) In a sense, what we are trying to find out is what percentage of the company has been put into hock.

If we find that 100 percent or more is in hock, then it's an automatic warning signal. The investors have essentially no equity and the company is sure to be having trouble paying interest payments from current income.

A more reasonable ratio is 50 percent. (In other than low-priced stocks, a ratio of about 35 percent is advised, but small start-up companies often have higher costs.)

Liabilitiespressure

This is a quick test to determine solvency. To use it, however, we need the most up-to-the-minute information. We need to know *current* liabilities and *current* assets.

Assets have to be greater than liabilities. If not, the company can't pay its bills tomorrow without borrowing. Sometimes companies will run cash short and have to undertake short-term borrowing to cover problems. If, however, the company already has a large long-term debt (see the previous discussion), this could be a critical problem.

Generally speaking, the greater current assets than current liabilities, the healthier the company.

Managementitis

This is the hardest of all problems to diagnose. Everyone knows that a company with bad management is ultimately not going to succeed. What no one knows is how to tell bad management from good.

I have seen advisers insist that potential investors thoroughly investigate a company's management. How does one do this? Can you trust the findings of brokers or consultants who claim to have investigated the management? (My experience has been you can't trust outside opinion on this subject further than you can throw it.) Have you the time to call the managers and talk with them? And if you do, what will you learn?

For myself I have developed three little tests for management's abilities. It really has nothing to do with examining what management has done in the past. (After all, how can we judge if a success or failure was due to management or some other cause?) This information can often be found out from a call to a broker (if he or she has done his or her homework) or by a call to a manager at the company.

TEST 1—What's the turnover rate in management? If top or middle managers are turning over in less than eighteen months, there could be a problem. If it's less than six months, there *definitely* are suggestions of a problem. On the other hand, if the same team has been around for four or five years or more, what's wrong with them? Why aren't they moving up to bigger and better companies? You want management that's in the middle, that's been around for a while, but not too long.

TEST 2—How old is the management team? I mean two things. How old are they chronologically? If they are very young (fresh out of college), then chances are they are learning at the company. If they are very old, then maybe the company is their nest until they retire. We want someone who is still active, but not wet behind the ears.

Second, how long have they been in management? Five years? Ten years? Or six months? The more experience, the better.

TEST 3—Has management put its money where its mouth is? How much stock did the managers themselves buy? They undoubtedly received insider (Rule 144) stock. How much actual cash out-of-pocket was paid for it?

There are other health problems that can affect a company. But the most serious have been noted. Passing the health test should be a minimum requirement for any stock you are considering purchasing for its long-term growth.

6. Is the Economy Favorable?

There is an old wive's tale that goes something like, "The pennies are the first and the last to run."

What this means is that when the economy is coming out of a recession and starting to boom, the first to make a big move up are the pennies. Similarly, just as the economy is starting to take a downturn, the last stocks to make advances are the pennies.

The reason I call it an old wives' tale is that sometimes it just doesn't work. On the other hand, it works enough times not to be ignored. When it works, I think it works for these reasons. Coming out of a recession, many investors remain unsure. Are we really coming out? Or is it a false start? The serious money isn't yet willing to invest. Yet, many are willing to gamble small amounts. So the pennies get heavy attention.

Similarly, once the economy has expanded for a time, the serious money will get the jitters and stop investing, anticipating a downturn. At that time there will be many investors who don't believe it, who think the expansion will continue. They're willing to take a gamble on small amounts of money, so once again low-priced stocks move.

Of course, since there are numerous false turns during recessions and expansions, there are many runs for penny stocks. And, of course, sometimes the rule doesn't apply.

Nevertheless, it would be foolish not to see that there is sometimes a link and that it's important to track the economy.

Tracking the economy

This can be harder than it first appears to be. We are barraged on all sides with economic opinions, some good, some not quite so good, and some just plain terrible. If you're economically savvy, then you should be able to sort it out. If you're not, then here are three clues to help:

1. Watch interest rates. Stocks love low interest rates, hate high rates. (Watch the *trend* in rates, whether up or down, more than the current rate.)
2. Watch employment. Stocks love high employment, disdain low (although in recent years high stock prices have been sustained with historically high unemployment).
3. Watch the money supply. It's reported every Thursday. Big jumps today often portend higher inflation down the road. Stocks like low inflation, dislike high.

7. Is the Market Moving Up or Moving Down?

I really get tickled listening to the market reports on TV at the end of the day. Perhaps like me you've heard reporters say something like, "The market sold off today in response to fighting in Lebanon." Or perhaps the reporter said, "There was a big surge in buying, reacting to the release of money supply figures." Or, "Failure in Congress to pass the tax reform bill pushed the market down."

Now really, did that reporter talk to the "market" to get those conclusions? On an average day there might have been sixty to a hundred million shares traded on the New York Stock Exchange alone, let alone AMEX, NASDAQ, and other OTC stock. Does the reporter mean that in each of those trades, the determining element was a world crisis, the economy, or politics? How does he or she know?

The truth of the matter is, no one knows why the market is doing this or doing that, ever. The best we can hope to do is follow along and see trends long after they've developed.

This doesn't mean, of course, that we can ignore the market. If we recognize that the market is bearish (trending lower), then perhaps we ought to wait before buying (for lower prices), or sell now (to take advantage of what might be currently higher prices). Similarly, if the market is bullish (trending higher), then perhaps we ought to reverse our decisions.

The point is that we must spend some effort following the market. For the Big Board we might follow the Dow Jones Averages or the S&P 500. There are also separate indices for utilities and other types of stocks.

Of course, the logical question is, "How does the Dow or other Big Board index relate to the pennies?" The answer is that there is no direct relation. However, many investors and brokers do tend to look for a "trickle-down" effect, which takes about two to three months. In other words, what we see on the Dow today may be reflected in the pennies two to three months from today. (Again, this is just a rule of thumb. It's not set in granite.)

For low-priced stocks, we might also want to follow the indices listed in various publications. For example, shown opposite is the index for the past three years—as listed by the *OTC Stock Journal*.

Indices such as these should neither be ignored nor followed religiously. They should be watched and the information they provide factored in with other information and judgments.

One last point: I've frequently heard people say that "the market's always right." Usually what they mean is that marketplace determines price. It's not what you or I think the price should be, it's what the market says it is that counts.

That's all well and good as long as it's taken no further. But some new investors see it as saying that the market is a kind of guru that points to proper pricing. We'll say more about this in the next section on technical analysis. But suffice it to say that that market isn't right or wrong in this sense, it's just the market. At any moment it expresses the anticipations of all buyers and sellers as evidenced by their willingness to trade. That's it, nothing more. There's nothing mystical about it.

The market isn't smart or stupid. If you find seventeen reasons why it must do one thing, all I can guarantee is that the chances are at least fifty-fifty it will do the opposite. It doesn't think, it doesn't care. The less we think of it as being a personality, the better off we are.

Listen to advice, but don't rely on it

This is the last comment I have to make regarding the market and picking stocks. It's important to get the advice

OTC Stock Journal Composite Index, 1983–1986

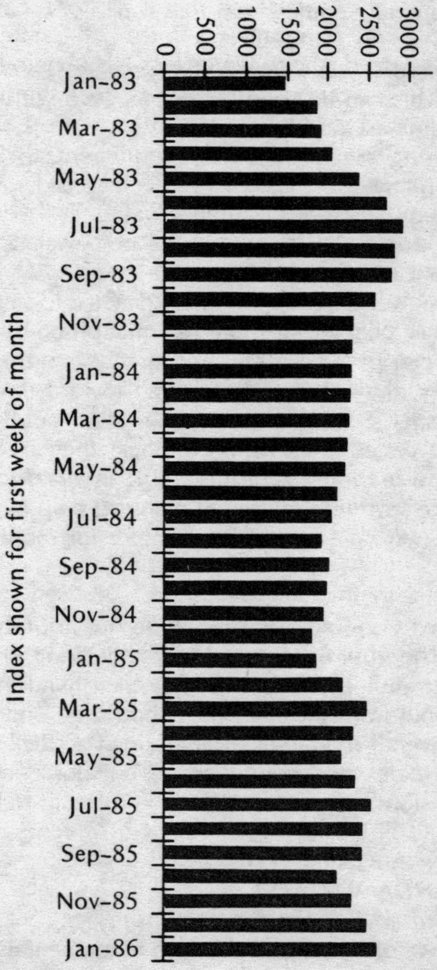

0 500 1000 1500 2000 2500 3000

Jan–83
Mar–83
May–83
Jul–83
Sep–83
Nov–83
Jan–84
Mar–84
May–84
Jul–84
Sep–84
Nov–84
Jan–85
Mar–85
May–85
Jul–85
Sep–85
Nov–85
Jan–86

Index shown for first week of month

of others, particularly those who have spent more time than we studying the market or a particular stock. This advice generally comes from four sources:

1. *Brokers (including their firms' research departments).* This can be good or bad, as we'll see in Chapter 11, "Finding a Good Broker."
2. *Rating Services.* These rate different stocks. Unfortunately, many of the companies we'll consider aren't regularly rated; hence, it's of limited value.
3. *Financial Advisories.* These are newsletters put out by different individuals around the country. At last count there were over a hundred of them devoted to stocks alone. (See the last chapter for more information on them.)

   These can provide useful and timely information. Unfortunately, they tend to be slanted toward the views of the publisher. Sometimes, however, those publishers also may have vested interests in the stocks they are touting.
4. *Newspapers, tabloids, and magazines.* These provide general information of a sort to help us in a general way. (Again, see the last chapter for more information.)

Now, why should you read these but not rely on their advice? The answer is that they really don't know, they may be prejudiced, they may have their hand in the till.

The input from these sources should be only one part of your overall fundamental analysis of a stock. It should give you clues and helpful hints, but don't let it make your decisions.

WHY FUNDAMENTALS?

These, then, are the seven different fundamentals to watch out for. As you can see, some apply in the form of tests to stock. Others (such as economic trends) are items you need to be ever aware of.

As you go through your investment life looking for growth stocks, try to remember these fundamentals. When a stock comes along that is sizzling hot with all kinds of appeal, try to step aside, count to ten, and consider. If you're really buying the stock for growth, how does it stack up fundamentally? If it doesn't cut it fundamentally, then you probably should look elsewhere.

HOW TO PLAY A STOCK

In advertising, it's common to look at two elements of any product with an eye toward marketing it. The first element involves the actual benefits the product offers: If it's a drug, what will it cure? If it's a candy, how sweet is it? If it's a car, is it reliable and comfortable? . . . and so forth. This is, so to speak, looking at the "meat" of it.

The other element in marketing, oftentimes considered even more important, is the "sizzle." How much "sex appeal" does the product have? Is it trendy? Does it catch the eye?

Sometimes virtually worthless products, such as common rocks or plastic hoops or simple dolls, can be marketed almost entirely on their sizzle. People want them, indeed fight to pay inflated sums of money to get them, because they are perceived as having great intangible value.

In penny stocks a similar situation prevails. In the last chapter we looked at the traditional method of finding winning stock—looking for growth. We approached stocks in a fundamental way—what was the P/E ratio, the book value, the price history, and so on? In essence, we were analyzing the "steak."

In this chapter, however, we're going to look at stock a different way. We are going to analyze the sizzle. We are going to see the effect popularity has on a stock.

Remember, here we're not concerned with fundamental analysis, which tries to determine true value. Instead we're concerned with perceived value.

PERCEIVED VALUE

This is a trickier notion to deal with than most people realize. Almost all of us would be in agreement as to value as determined in the previous chapter by a fundamental analysis. But what about value when there is no "steak?"

For example, consider high fashion. A dress in Penney's might cost fifty dollars. On the other hand, a dress by *Halston* might cost five thousand dollars. Fundamentally, this makes no sense. The material used in the five-thousand-dollar dress may not be much more valuable than the material used in the fifty-dollar dress. In addition, fashions change quickly. That dress for five thousand dollars today might be worthless by next season.

Yet, there is a market for the high-priced dress. In fact, buyers may be standing in line to get it. The reason is that the higher-priced dress is perceived to have fashion value, and for those who worship fashion, price is no object.

Something similar happens in penny stocks. Some stocks are perceived as having great value. They sizzle. They are fashionable, they catch the eye, they have sex appeal.

However they are described, the value of these stocks comes not from a fundamental analysis, but rather from a perception of value on the part of the buyers. (Of course, if the stocks have fundamental strength, then all the better, but that's last chapter's story.)

AN EXAMPLE OF SIZZLE

For example, as this is being written, there are at least half a dozen low-priced stock companies in the United States that are coming out with medical products that purport to either cure, treat, or test for the disease AIDS (Acquired Immune Deficiency Syndrome).

This is good timing because also as of this writing, there is great concern and even downright fear among the general population regarding this disease, and any product that promises relief is welcomed. (Of course, by the time you read this, the disease may have vanished or may be an epidemic. But the point here is with regard to its effect on stock, not on health.)

In almost every case the stock of those companies with AIDS-related products is doing very well. The question we need to ask is, why?

Well, obviously if these companies do indeed have beneficial products, those products will be extremely valuable and the stock will be in great demand. This is the fundamental approach.

However, I would be willing to wager that ninety-nine out of a hundred investors who bought stock in these companies did *no* fundamental analysis of any kind. In fact, without knowing anything about those companies and just given the history of small pharmaceutical companies in general that purport to have miracle drugs, I would be surprised if any of them ever came to market with a product, let alone actually came up with something successful.

In other words, the *idea* of an AIDS-related product is what counts, not necessarily the product itself. The concept has sizzle, it has investment sex appeal, it catches the eye, it's fashionable. Hence, the concept has perceived value; many investors will buy the stock and, at least temporarily, this may boost the stock's price.

INVESTOR SAVVY

Does this suggest that these investors are somehow fools or ignoramuses? Hardly, they are probably being very shrewd. They see an opportunity and they are playing it. They have bought a popular stock, gambling that its popularity will increase and that they will be able to sell before it peaks. They may hold it a few days, weeks, or months until it has run its course. Along the way, they hope, speculation will have forced the price up until they can sell at a handsome profit.

This is what I mean by playing a stock.

The investors here are not interested in looking for growth. They are only interested in speculating on price. The smart player will determine which stocks have the best perceived value and ride with those as long as they are winners.

WHEN THE CRASH COMES

Of course, these speculative bubbles don't last forever. Sometimes they only last a few days. Other times they last for as long as six months. But eventually they burst.

Perhaps the company is forced to make an announcement that initial testing of its product was "inconclusive."

In other words, it doesn't work. Or maybe there is the positive announcement by another company of a true cure. Or maybe the illness itself suddenly disappears and the need for the product vanishes.

For whatever the reason, the sizzle suddenly goes away. And without sizzle, there is no support for these stocks, so they plummet in price. Of course, the smart investor has long since moved on.

It's important to note that I'm not suggesting that all companies whose products have sizzle have no fundamental value. Ideally a stock will have *both* steak *and* sizzle. However, in the penny stock market, even if it's mostly just sizzle, the smart investor can still profit.

LOOKING FOR THE SIZZLE

With regard to penny stocks, finding stocks with sizzle requires technical analysis. (The term "technical analysis" here has a slightly different meaning than with regard to higher-priced stocks, as we'll see shortly.)

For low-priced stock a technical analysis means determining which stock is going to make a big move for other than fundamental reasons.

No field is exempt from these speculative bubbles. In the recent past we saw it happen in low-priced oil stocks (exploration as well as development) in the seventies, in gold and silver mining stocks in the early eighties, and in many start-up pharmaceuticals involved with genetic engineering in the mid-eighties. Along the way we had excitement in robotics and in computers (both widely considered "dead" as of this writing).

Hundreds of companies, some no more than shells, got involved in these fields at the height of the excitement. In many cases their stocks soared, at least temporarily. And those investors who bought wisely and sold timely did indeed do very well.

HOW TO PLAY A STOCK

In general, I've found that those who did succeed in playing stocks followed at least these three rules:

1. They picked companies on the basis of the sex appeal (sizzle) of their products.
2. They bought at the beginning of the popularity curve and sold immediately at the sign of any drop in price.
3. They sold when the stock reached a predetermined level (for example, twice, three times, or whatever the original price).

Of course, a fourth rule was that they adhered strictly to the first three. We'll discuss picking a stock in a few paragraphs, but first a few words about rules 2 and 3.

SELLING

When playing a stock, it's important to keep focused on what you're doing. *You are speculating*. Nothing more, nothing less. That means you're not looking for long-term growth, you're not going to get personally attached to the stock. The only time you can win when playing a stock (we'll talk about selling short, another way of winning, in a later chapter) is by dumping the losers.

Determining a loser on a stock *play* is easy. If it goes down in value, it's a loser. Usually a drop of 10 percent in value is a sufficient indication.

A player who hangs on to a "played" stock that drops is going to be a big loser. Remember, these stocks were bought for sizzle, not for steak. They probably don't have the fundamental strength to rebound from a loss. Once they start down, it's a sure sign that they've run out of sizzle. Now it's only a quick trip to the bottom and out for most of them.

Sell, sell, sell—the three most important words to remember when playing a stock that goes down in price.

On the other hand, you want to hang on to your winners. You've got a stock that's got plenty of sizzle, you got in at the right time, and it's moving up fast. How long do you hold it?

Obviously, you hold it as long as it's going up. But that's hard to judge. A speculative penny stock can peak and plummet in value in a day, in hours—much faster, in general, than most nonprofessional investors can react.

Therefore, shrewd investors have arbitrary limits they establish. The exact nature of these limits isn't critical. What is critical is that you have them.

THE LIMITS FOR A TYPICAL PLAY

Here are the rules by which one investor I know limits her stock plays:

"When the stock doubles, I will sell half. I will then have my original investment out and still have half the stock I purchased.

"I will then hold this until the stock doubles again and again sell half. I will continue to do this as long as the stock goes up.

"In any event, as soon as it drops ten percent from its previous high, I will immediately sell all shares I own."

These limits don't guarantee she'll win. But they at least give her a fighting chance at not losing.

PICKING THE STOCKS TO PLAY

This is certainly the most difficult part of playing a stock. The reason is that even within a hot field, some stocks will do well while others fare poorly. We want to get the former. There are five suggestions I have:

1. Be Sure the Field Has Sizzle.

This is the prerequisite for playing a stock. I don't care whether it's robotics, frozen yogurt, drugs, or hair growth. The field has to have sex appeal.

This isn't hard to judge. Look around you. What do people want? What are they afraid of? Who is offering solutions? Answer these three questions and you have the sizzle field for the moment.

Of course, there's always confirmation. Check with any low-priced stockbroker. He or she will instantly be able to confirm which field is hot.

CAUTION: Fields lose their sizzle very quickly. One big mistake in playing stocks that many new investors make is going into yesterday's field. To win here, you've got to get in at the beginning.

2. Find the Stock That the Technicians Recommend.

Technical analysts love charts. These charts invariably show the months, days, or weeks along the bottom axis and the price of a stock (or group of stocks) along the vertical axis. The price is a sawtooth moving up and down in the market.

Technicians draw lines on these charts frequently, connecting the price tops or price bottoms. By doing this they identify such things as "resistance levels" (a price through which a stock will have trouble passing either up or down) or "breakout points" (a price figure that, if attained by a stock, means it will continue to move some distance in whatever direction it has been going).

If you're into astrology, you'll love technicians. They can come up with a prediction for anything. What's more, frequently they're right!

Just as myths and legends are frequently the remnants of the dead science and religion of former civilizations lingering on in the present, so, too, is technical analysis the lingering judgment connected with former market events. Technicians look at the past and try to predict the future.

Beware the "science" of technical analysis

Regardless of how much chartists may disagree, there *is no science of technical analysis.* Rather, it is only subjective interpretation, much as reading entrails was for the ancient Greeks and Romans.

But, just as voodoo and witch doctoring sometimes work, so, too, does technical analysis sometimes work, and for that reason it cannot be ignored. As is said about witch doctors and voodoo, that they work because some believe in them, so it may be true of technical analysis.

A technician says a stock must do this or that, and perhaps it happens *because* the technician said it would. Maybe it's a self-fulfilling prophecy.

It makes no difference. When playing a stock, listen to the technical analysis. Get a readout on the field (to be sure it's beginning, not ending, and does have sizzle) and the stock (to be sure it's a leader in the field).

Finding technical analysis

Where do you get technical analysis? Start with your stockbroker. In my experience, while they *all* profess to carefully evaluate the fundamentals of a stock, nine out of ten don't make their decisions based on fundamentals.

Talk to brokers, ask them why they think this or that, and when you start hearing terms such as "tops" and "bottoms" and "rising lines" and "resistance" and "breakout," you know you're getting technical analysis.

Be polite and ask them their sources and check it out. There's no better way to find a sizzling stock than to follow a technician to it.

On the other hand, the broker may simply be following the company line and have no idea what technical theory is. If that's the case, then your next bet is to find a broker or an underwriter who does know the theory and go with him or her.

3. Pick a Company That Has a No-Fail Product.

You know the kind. The world is crazy for dolls. This company has just come out with a doll that is the central character of a hit movie of the same name. The doll has been test-marketed in three major malls in different cities and kids waited an average of one and a half hours just to get it. In addition, it is being endorsed by a Saturday morning cartoon idol. How can it lose?

It probably can't, as long as the field has sizzle. Even if the doll is a dud, the strength of the field itself should carry it along for some profits. The product is "no-fail."

4. Look for Management with Sizzle.

Look for stars, names that ring bells. Ideally you want someone who has been a winner before.

There are some classic cases here, not always limited

to penny stocks. Consider Lee A. Iacocca and Chrysler. Or a low-priced stock example, PaperBack Software, led by Adam Osborne, whose reputation remained untarnished even after his Osborne Computer company failed. His name alone was sufficient to initially promote the stock.

5. Always Look for a Little Steak.

Playing a stock is like getting a fever. If it's a mining stock, it's "gold fever." If it's a computer stock, it's "high-tech fever." It's contagious, and once you get it, it's hard to lose. Getting a fever for gold stocks can make you feverish for high tech, for pharmaceuticals, for the whole spectrum. It can cloud overall judgment.

The best way to avoid these fevers is, once you've picked a group of stocks you're considering playing (say a dozen), to try a fundamental analysis of each. All other things being equal, go with the stock that has the best fundamentals. It's the way to put a little sanity into what is admittedly a wild and sometimes wicked field.

BOTTOM LINE

Remember, when you play a stock, you are speculating, gambling. It's risky and you won't always win. You're shooting for the moon and you hope to retire on your winnings, so don't complain if you get shot down quite a few times before you have any success.

WINNING WITH NEW ISSUES

When some investors speak of penny stocks, what they are really talking about are new issues. New issues are undoubtedly the fastest way to make (or lose) money in penny stocks. Prices here shoot up or tumble, often in days. If you're on the winning side, you can make a fortune. Or, if your timing is bad, you could lose a great deal.

WHAT IS A NEW ISSUE?

A new issue is *new* stock issued by a company. Although it could be an addition to existing public stock already offered by the company, in most cases with low-priced stock, what we're speaking of is the first issue. In other words, we have a private company. Now it's going public, and in the process it is issuing stock.

Regardless of what you may already know about new issues, there are at least three important facts that must be remembered when we are dealing with low-priced stock:

1. Typically the *total value* of the new issue is low. Under two million dollars is common. A million to half a million is not unusual. This means we are dealing with a *thin* market. While there may be a great many shares because of the low cost (a few cents per share), the total money raised is not great, meaning that any one wealthy individual or company theoretically can corner and influence the stock (see the next chapter).

2. Virtually all new issue stock must have Securities and Exchange Commission approval. BUT THIS APPROVAL IS NOT A RECOMMENDATION—IN MOST CASES THERE IS NO GOVERNMENT DETERMINATION OF MERIT ON NEW ISSUES. There are exceptions, of course, as in the case where in addition to the SEC, a stock is issued in a state that makes a merit determination. But in most cases, no official body has said this is a good company and the offering is a good investment. In terms of quality, it's strictly a case of caveat emptor, let the buyer beware.

3. Most of the money made on new issues is made on the first *day* or within the first few weeks of issue. This means that the shrewd investors try to buy the new issues, then try to get out as quickly as possible after the stock starts trading.

Finally, it's fair to say that although the new issues market is risky, it is also potentially quite profitable. Having said that, let's see how it works and where the money can be made.

WHY ARE THERE NEW ISSUES?

You are a chemist working for a large photographic company. In your garage in your spare time you work on new ways to create emulsions. One day you stumble on a process for creating a "fast" (highly receptive) photographic film *that does not use silver* as part of the process.

Chemists have been working unsuccessfully for eighty years trying to develop this process, but you think you have stumbled onto the key to it. What you need is time to conduct some more experiments.

So you contact several friends—one is a lawyer, another an accountant, yet a third is in manufacturing. You explain what you've found and they are enthusiastic. You look around and see that each partner is an expert in an area vital to success if the product is ever to reach market. "Hmm," you think, "this could be the start of something big!"

Each of you puts up $10,000 and you form a corporation. You quit your job at the photographic company and use the money to live on while you work full-time in your garage.

After six months the money is gone. You're convinced the process will work, as soon as you get a few glitches out of it. But that will take time and more money. So you get a second mortgage on your house and come up with $25,000. One way or another, each of your partners does likewise. Now you open a small research and development office in a local industrial park.

It goes slowly, but eight months later, just as the money is about gone, you make it work! Of course, you've only done it in a few experimental situations. Now you need the money to rent a large plant and start making film on a mass scale. Once you do this, you can either market the film yourself or sell out for what will probably be hundreds of millions to a big photographic company.

But you need a million dollars, cash, to get off the ground. Where are you going to get it?

You and your partners have exhausted your cash and

all your other personal reserves. The bank won't touch your scheme since you have no collateral. Venture capitalists will consider it, but only if you give them 90 percent ownership.

What do you do?

You decide to go public and issue stock.

You call every stockbroker you know and eventually one firm agrees to handle, or underwrite, your offering, and you're on your way. (We'll get into the actual process of underwriting new stock in a few pages.)

WHERE THE PROFIT IS

What we've been seeing is the great American way of raising capital to start a new business. It's been done over and over since this country was founded, and many of the largest corporations got their start in this fashion. It's stretching to grasp a dream.

Let's continue the scenario. When your *company's* stock finally gets to market, investors will analyze it. The underwriter who is promoting it will add hype such as, "A revolutionary product," "It could be a new Kodak or Xerox," "A chance to get in on the ground floor of tomorrow's Fortune 500 company." This is the sizzle we were talking about.

In this case investors are probably going to be very excited. You have experiments to show that the product actually works. The potential is enormous. Word spreads and investors start calling asking for stock. The offering is quickly gobbled up (all the shares offered are sold).

After all the new issues are sold, the stock starts trading. Note: Up until now there has been no trading of the stock. Instead, there have been a set number of shares offered for sale through the underwriter and his associates.

Once the stock is actually issued, however, a trading market begins (the after market). Those who bought the new issues may want to sell. Those who didn't get in on the ground floor may now want to buy.

Demand is heavy for the stock on the first day of trading. It opens at ten cents a share and quickly moves to twenty cents. Within three days it is up to thirty cents.

Now let's stop the scenario. Who's made money so far and where?

WHERE THE MONEY IS

1. The investors who bought the new issue (for ten cents a share) before it began trading have tripled their money, if they sell immediately.
2. The underwriter who issued the stock was paid a commission by the company and probably has made a substantial profit in addition on the trading.
3. Investors who bought on the first day at a low price and have ridden the stock up have made a considerable profit if they now sell.

These three groups have made money. But then, on the fourth day of trading, the photographic company where you, the inventor, formerly worked brings suit against you. It says you developed your revolutionary process while working for it, hence technically the process belongs to it.

You say the suit is without merit and demand to know why your lawyer partner didn't foresee this. He says he's a real estate lawyer; how should he know about patent suits?

The suit seeks to tie up all your funds from the stock issue, so you can't begin manufacturing the product further until the court settles the dispute. Your funds are wide open in easily accessed accounts. You ask your accountant partner why he didn't foresee this and shield the funds.

He says he's just an accountant who prepares 1040 tax returns in April. How could he know this was going to happen?

You turn to your partner whose expertise is in manufacturing and he shrugs his shoulders. He says he can tell someone how to operate a lathe, but what does he know about this high finance?

That day your stock drops to five cents a share. Within a month it's down to a penny. Two months later you file for Chapter 11 bankruptcy and no broker will handle your stock anymore.

Now, once again, who's made money?

WHERE THE MONEY'S GONE

1. The investors who bought the issue *and sold* almost immediately in the after market.

2. The underwriter (provided he didn't get stuck with a lot of your stock).

3. The investors who bought immediately and then quickly *resold* in the after market.

In other words, anyone who bought early and sold quickly made money, perhaps a great deal of money. Who lost money? Anyone who bought your company's stock and held it for future growth.

IN THE REAL WORLD

The preceding example (which is probably much closer to real life than many brokers would care to admit) illustrates where profits are made in new issues. The company has a dream. That dream is hyped by the underwriter. And investors buy in.

In many cases what investors are buying is 90 percent or more sizzle. When that's the case, the way to win is to get in as early and as low as possible and then get out as quickly as possible after the stock has moved up. (This strategy has a down side, of course. If you get out too early, you chance losing out if the stock turns out to be a real long-term winner, a stock that happens to have some steak as well as sizzle. To compensate, some investors will always keep a portion of each winning new issue for the long term, just in case.)

Of course, things don't usually happen quite as fast as in our example. A new company may have a trial period of six months or more in which to succeed or fail. The underwriter may support the stock for a variety of reasons for quite some time. (See the chapter on underwriter pitfalls.) Nevertheless, from the investor's viewpoint, speed is of the essence here. *Most* new companies fail. Once investors smell failure, it's usually too late to dump the stock.

WHEN THE MARKET SIZZLES

When there's a lot of interest in the penny stock market, almost any new issue has a good chance of going up in value the first few days on the after market, particularly if it has a strong underwriter. Therefore, investors scramble to get these issues as early and as low as possible. (It's a different story in a cold market—there, particularly if there are too many new issues coming out, many may open down the first few days.)

A sizzling market presents some problems for investors. Frequently in such a market, it is hard to get new issues. Everyone wants them; hence, there aren't enough to go around. What you need here is a good broker. (See Chapter 11 for how to find one.)

Additionally, in a sizzling market, scoundrels have a tendency to come in and start up hopeless companies just to profit from issuing virtually worthless new stock. (Remember, the SEC requires *full disclosure*. It normally doesn't comment on merit.)

And underwriters—who are well aware that investors often don't care a hoot if the company has a chance or not for success, but just want in and out quick—are sometimes tempted to promote less than promising companies and then to undertake devious if not downright illegal methods to support the stock in the after market. A hot market breeds all kinds of problems. We'll cover pitfalls in the next chapter.

The important thing to remember is speed. In most cases when the market's got everyone talking, new issue profits are made by getting in early and selling quick. Also, remember the exception to this rule. I bought new issue stock years ago that I am still holding to this day. It turned out to be that rare breed of a fundamentally good company. Always keep a watchful eye out for the company that has both sizzle and steak.

HOW TO FIND OUT ABOUT NEW ISSUES

There are essentially three sources. The first is the broker. A good broker will keep you informed of what's coming out.

Second, there are the advisories. We noted these in Chapter 5. Many of them list *all* new stock issues in registration. Some of them are devoted exclusively to picking the best of the new issues.

Finally, there is word of mouth. As you get more familiar with the field and as those in the field get to know you, you'll begin getting phone calls telling you about this new issue or that.

HOW TO SELECT THE BEST NEW ISSUES

Obviously, some companies are better than others. Not all will have troubles such as those seen in our previous example. Some will go forward and may eventually become the IBMs of tomorrow. As elsewhere, therefore, if buying new issues is your cup of tea, it's important that you aim for the best quality stock you can get.

When buying new issues, I have found that there are three rules that are particularly helpful:

1. Don't waste time chasing unavailable stock.
2. Get a reliable broker who does his homework.
3. Know the process.

With regard to the first rule, it's simply the case that on any given day there are probably upwards of twenty new issues available. The biggest mistake is to focus in on only one and desperately try to get that stock. If you can't get one new issue, aim for another. There are always plenty out there. Waiting for that impossible dream means you'll probably lose out.

The second rule is also vital. It's the broker who's going to get you the new issues. If the broker you're using can't get good new issues for you, you need a new broker. We'll cover this in greater detail in Chapter 11.

Finally, there's the matter of understanding the process of issuing new stocks.

KNOW WHAT'S HAPPENING

If you're already an experienced low-priced stock investor, you may want to skip to the next section. But if you're new to the field, you should find some valuable information here.

The process of coming out with new issue stock is really not that complex, although it is fairly rigid. There are some things that must be done and others that must be avoided. And there are a number of factors that end up affecting you, the future buyer.

Probably the best way to learn is to follow a new stock to market. Here are the steps involved:

1. The Company Decides It Needs New Capital.

In our earlier example of a photo company, the capital was to go for setting up manufacturing. This is typical. Most often companies that go public have already done the research and development. Now they need funds to get their product ready for market.

2. The Company May Try a "Private Placement."

This means selling stock to individuals or companies that specialize in taking risks on new ventures. If this works, they may still go public later if they need more money.

3. The Company Decides to Go Public and Looks for an Underwriter.

An underwriter is an entity that will undertake to help move the offering through the various legal steps to market, then offer the stock to the public, and then (usually) handle the stock in the after market as a market maker. Most brokerage houses that specialize in penny stocks also underwrite new issues.

The importance of the underwriter

The first critical step for the *company*, therefore, is getting a good underwriter. As it turns out, this is also a critical step for the investor. Some underwriters over the long haul have brought out one excellent offering after another. Other houses have brought out one piece of junk stock after another.

In choosing an underwriter, the *company* usually has as its goal finding a brokerage house that has a track record of offering successful new issues. Since investors sometimes shop underwriters before companies (for reasons that should be evident from the previous paragraphs), this is the surest way to get a successful offering. The *company* owners will now begin knocking on doors trying to get the best underwriter.

From the underwriter's viewpoint, this is a time-consuming and often bothersome process. In a sizzling market, top underwriters say they get proposals from a hundred companies for each one they seriously consider. And they only accept one out of each twenty they consider.

The odds, therefore, of getting a strong underwriter do not favor the *company*. Nevertheless, if the *company* is strong and it and/or its product has sizzle, underwriters will pay attention.

Eventually an underwriter agrees to work with the *company*. From its perspective, the underwriter, in making the decision to handle a stock, is expected to protect investors by thoroughly investigating the *company* to make sure that it is a good and safe investment. This "due diligence" investigation should be such that the underwriter is convinced that the *company* is good enough for the underwriter itself to buy the stock.

(Unfortunately, my experience has been that while some underwriters are indeed extremely diligent, others are not. While some try to bring only public companies that have the best chance to succeed, others seem more involved in companies that offer the highest profit to the underwriter. Also, unfortunately, this problem appears not to reside only with the small underwriters, nor only with those that just occasionally put out successful issues.)

Of course, it all comes down to the investors. Experienced investors know a good underwriter is probably more responsible for pushing a company's stock than the company. An underwriter that has a track record of six successful new issues is going to be much in demand by investors. (To find such underwriters, check into Chapter 5, "Investment Advisories.")

4. The Underwriter Lines Up the Sales Team.

The underwriter might handle the entire sale of the stock itself, if it is strong enough. In many cases, however, the underwriter puts together a syndicate that includes other brokerage houses that will act as market makers and brokers, which may also handle sale of the new issue.

5. A Proposal Is Presented to the SEC.

This proposal, prepared by the *company,* usually with the underwriter's help, is in the form of a registration statement. It describes the *company,* its officers, the business of the *company,* the plan for offering the new issues, the potential risks involved, and many other important facts. The SEC will examine this material to make sure that all facts, good and bad, have been disclosed. As noted, the SEC does not judge the merit of the offering, only whether or not proper procedure has been followed and whether there is outright fraud involved in the stock sale.

6. State Registration Is Sought.

The team also submits registration proposals to the states in which the new issue stock will be sold. It's important to understand that in addition to SEC registration, new issues must be registered in every state in which they are sold.

This can be a far more complex and difficult process than getting SEC registration. The reason is that the laws for registration differ state by state. In addition, many states not only pass judgment on whether all items are disclosed, but they also render merit judgments on whether or not the stock is a sound investment. In merit states, getting approval can be a very long and difficult process.

Almost always, therefore, new issues are not registered in all states in the country, but rather only in those that have short and nonmerit registration processes. This is called "blue-skying" the stock.

As of this writing, those states in which new issues are most commonly registered include:

Colorado
Connecticut
Delaware
Florida
Illinois
Maryland
Nevada
New Jersey
New York
Washington, D.C.

Blue-sky states

It's important to understand that *an underwriter or a broker cannot legitimately sell you a new issue stock unless you are a resident of a state in which the stock is registered.*

Of course, people are always finding ways to buy new issues out-of-state. Frequently people maintain an address in a registered state in order to be able to get stock. Some individuals buy stock through relatives or friends residing in a registered state.

In any event, getting clearance by the states is necessary before stock can be sold.

7. A Prospectus Is Issued.
This essentially reveals everything that was submitted to the SEC. It describes the *company* and the principal officers. It indicates the product or service the *company* is going to offer and it outlines the risks involved.

The initial prospectus will have stamped in red on its cover a notice that SEC approval for issue of the stock has not yet been given. These are sometimes called "red herring" prospectuses. (We'll have a more detailed explanation of the prospectus later in the chapter.)

8. A "Quiet Period" Occurs.
From the time registration starts until ninety days after the stock has been cleared for sale by the SEC, no one involved in the sale may make any statements other than those contained in the prospectus. If anyone involved with the stock issue should make contradictory statements or add information other than that contained in the prospectus, it might be deemed misleading and the SEC could halt the sale.

Should there be some significant changes affecting the *company* that must be publicized, then these must be attached by "stickering" (adding them on a sticker) to each prospectus.

9. Stock Sales Start.
Within three days after the SEC gives approval for sale of the stock, the underwriter, brokers, and the sales team may start selling it. They normally have a maximum period of ninety days in which to sell out the issue.

10. Terms of Sale.

The new issue can be sold in one of two ways. The first way is termed "all or nothing." It is fairly self-descriptive. During the sales period all of the stock offered must be sold. If it is not sold, then all of the investors' money must be returned and there is no new issue.

The second way a stock can be sold is "minimum/maximum." In a mini/maxi there is a minimum amount of stock that must be sold before the issue can go forth. If this minimum isn't reached, then investors' money is returned. On the other hand, if interest is great, there is a maximum number of shares that may be sold in the sale period. No more than this number may be sold.

In addition, the sale itself can be handled in two ways. The most common method is for the underwriter to make a "best efforts" attempt at selling the stock. The underwriter will contact all brokers and associates possible in an attempt to get the widest possible distribution for the stock. In other words, the underwriter will use its best efforts to get a new issue sold out. However, if those efforts happen not to be enough, then the new stock doesn't get to market.

On the other hand, in some cases the underwriter may make a guarantee. This guarantee takes the form of the underwriter agreeing to buy up all the shares of the new issue. The underwriter in turn will then resell them. In a firm commitment a sellout is assured.

11. Syndication.

As noted earlier, in many cases more than one brokerage house will underwrite and sell the stock. Usually this is the case when there is a very large new issue or the underwriter doesn't have that much retail muscle. The term "syndicate" usually just means all those involved in the sale of the new issue.

Another reason for syndication is to bring more market makers in on the deal. This spreads the stock out and tends to heighten interest in it. Also, sometimes houses may "scratch each other's backs." They may carry an "average" new issue for the chance to be in on the action of a "hot" new issue.

12. Warrants and Units.

Many companies offering new issues will do so in "units." This consists of both stock and "warrants." A "warrant" is the right but not the obligation to buy additional stock at a set price until a set future date.

There are really two separate reasons a company might try to sell units instead of simply stock. The first is sales appeal. With stock alone, the buyer simply gets the certificates he purchases and that's it. With a unit, he gets the stock plus a warrant allowing him to buy additional stock up to a future date.

To see why this is appealing to investors, let's say the *company* offers units at fifty cents, which include two shares of stock and one warrant to buy an additional share of stock for fifty cents within six months of the offering.

If an investor buys a thousand units for five hundred dollars, he now has two thousand shares of stock plus warrants for an additional thousand. Further, let's say the stock does very well out of the starting gate and within a month is up to seventy-five cents a share.

If the investor were to buy more stock on the market, it would cost seventy-five cents a share. But he can exercise the warrant and buy it for fifty cents. There's a neat profit to be turned by simply selling the warrant. That's why investors like them.

Companies like units (stocks plus warrants) because it means they get capital initially when the stock is first issued and then again a second time if the stock's price goes up.

Warrants can be bought and sold on the market just like stocks. Their price is really a function of three separate factors:

1. *Time*. How much time to their expiration date? The more time until that date, the greater the opportunity for the price of the stock to move up and the more valuable the warrant.

2. *Intrinsic Value*. This is the difference between the price of the warrant and the price of the stock. In the preceding example, the intrinsic value was twenty-five cents. Of course, should the stock have gone down, then there could be a negative intrinsic value.

3. *Volatility*. This is the perception by the buying public of how volatile the stock is. If investors perceive that the stock behind the warrant is heading for the moon, then the warrant's price is going to be higher. If, on the other hand, they think it's getting ready to crash, the warrant's price will be affected adversely.

Finally, it is worth noting that sometimes companies will use units in an attempt to sell unpopular stock. The company says in effect, "We know you don't like our stock. So we're offering a bargain. Not only do you get our stock, but we'll throw in warrants as well."

The rejoinder should be, "If I don't like your stock, why should I like it better if you offer me more of it via warrants?" Besides, sometimes the price of units is jacked up over what the new issue would be if plain stock were offered.

13. The Prospectus.
Finally we come to the prospectus. Except for the actual sale, the biggest step in the process of bringing the stock to market for the *company* (although often the first step for the investor) is presenting the prospectus. If you're

considering buying a new issue, your broker will hand over a booklet to you and suggest that you look it over carefully. He or she may even add something such as, "It contains everything you should know about the company."

Indeed, however, it's frequently written in six-point type and it may be a hundred or more pages long. The prospectus may very well be the key to separating the winning stocks from the losers. But it's a key that's hard to use.

We are put on our guard right from the beginning by the standard disclaimer written in very large type: THIS MATERIAL HAS NEITHER BEEN APPROVED NOR DISAPPROVED BY THE SEC NOR HAS THE COMMISSION PASSED UPON THE ACCURACY OR ADEQUACY OF THE PROSPECTUS.

Remember, the SEC doesn't judge merits. It is basically concerned with disclosure.

READING THE PROSPECTUS

Well then, having discovered that what's easiest to read in the prospectus is the disclaimer, what are the important things to read? What should we concentrate on?

An honest answer is, "Everything."

However, there are some things I look at before others. Before beginning the following list, please understand that it is neither complete nor comprehensive. There are many other vital items to consider besides those noted here. I'm only indicating my preference for the order in which I consider items. My order of preference is as follows:

1. Management.

The prospectus should list the main officers of the company. It should give their background and experience. It should state how and why they are fit to handle the particular position they hold.

I look for age (Are they mature enough to handle the job?), past experience (Have they *successfully* done it before?), and background. This last can be fascinating. When the penny stock market was sizzling about a year ago, I came across a number of prospectuses that had the most interesting management. In each case several of the top positions were filled by people who had previously been in jail. It makes you stop and wonder.

2. Dilution.

This tells you what you are actually getting for your money. Novice investors sometimes make an erroneous assumption regarding new issues. They assume, for example, that if two million new shares are being issued at a dollar a share, then each share they buy represents one two-millionth interest in the company. Or, to put it another way, after the stock is sold, the total value of the company is the total value of the stock—$2 million. Nothing could be further from the truth.

What's being forgotten is the interest in the company that the founders have. They may be giving up some interest when they sell new issues, but they surely aren't giving it all up. In fact, often they may be giving up less than half. The total value of the new issues may be less than half of the total shares outstanding. For me, this becomes the primary issue with regard to dilution.

To see how this works, let's take an example. The *company* decides to make a public offering. The *company* currently has ten insiders, officers, and board of directors members who have ownership. Between them they have three million shares, for which they originally put up a total of $250,000.

The *company* has decided to issue two million new

shares at fifty cents apiece. The total raised will be $1 million, of which the company will receive $750,000 after paying the commissions for the sale of the new stock.

All of this information is revealed in the prospectus. Now, there are at least three questions the prospective investor must ask with respect to dilution:

What is the dilution?

This is actually a question that relates to the book value of the stock. I don't think it's that critical, especially since there are other questions of more importance, which we'll consider next. However, for those who do think book value is vital, here's how it's calculated:

We find the dilution of book value by adding the total old book value to the new capital (proceeds) from the sale, and dividing the sum by the total number of shares available after the sale. The equation looks like this:

$$\text{NEW BOOK VALUE} = \frac{\text{TOTAL BOOK VALUE} + \text{NEW CAPITAL}}{\text{TOTAL SHARES}}$$

For the *company* we'll assume that total old book value was $100,000. (Remember, total book value is found by taking tangible assets and subtracting all liabilities and debts.) Since we know the new capital and total shares, we can proceed right to the equation:

$$\$.17 = \frac{\$100{,}000 + \$750{,}000\ (= \$850{,}000)}{5{,}000{,}000\text{ shares}}$$

In other words, in this particular new issue the investor is putting up fifty cents to get a share of stock with a book value of seventeen cents. In terms of book value, this amounts to an immediate loss of 66 percent. For those readers who like to buy according to the book value, look elsewhere!

Of course, we need to be realistic. Most of the book value is the new capital. If it's used wisely, it can very quickly turn into earnings and new assets, which can jump the book value of the company. If it's used poorly, it can be dissipated and the book value can drop to zero.

New issues are a risk and this is where it is. But we knew there was risk coming in, so we shouldn't be too shocked when we see dilution.

How many total shares outstanding are there, and what is the relationship of new shares to old?

In this case, after the sale of the new issue, there will be five million shares outstanding, of which *all* the new investors will own two million while the original ten insiders will own three million. The old shareholders will control the company with 60 percent of the stock.

Who has voting rights? Who will control the company? In this case it's going to be the original ten investors. If *all* the new investors got together in a voting block, they still wouldn't outnumber (in terms of shares) the original investors. Am I comfortable with this?

Who has what at risk?

I had an old English professor who once told me, "If you want to analyze a play, look to motive. See why the characters are doing what they do." Much of the same holds true here.

What the new investors have at risk is obvious, the $1 million put up to buy the new issue. But what do the original investors, the insiders, have at risk?

In this case, they have invested $250,000. Having already risked that amount of money, what are they now inclined to do with a new infusion of $750,000? If the company is solid and there is a marketable product on the way, they may be inclined to use it to develop the company. On the other hand, they could take it and run. (To put it nicely, pay themselves high salaries until it's all gone.)

In this example, since the new investors are putting up much more cash than the original investors, it would be wise to now turn to that part of the prospectus that details where the new money is to go.

3. Use for Proceeds.

We would expect the prospectus to outline what the money raised is to be used for. I like to pay attention to specifics here. How much is going to salaries? Big salaries take funds away from the product.

Is there a specific plan for putting out a product? Is there a timetable? Are specific sums of money to be spent at specific times to implement the plan?

I like to see a company with a reasonable plan and with a timetable.

On the other hand, I have seen prospectuses that baldly state that there is no product envisioned, no timetable for developing one, and the money is to go as salary to the officers of the company while they dream up something to produce! Incredible, but it's there in black and white in the prospectus, if we read it.

I also like to pay particular attention to existing debts. How much of the proceeds is going to pay them off?

4. Is the Company Overburdened by Debts?

I have seen companies get into trouble by borrowing too much. They may have a terrific product, but bad management. They tried to bring it to market themselves, borrowed to do it, and failed. Now they are having a public offering to try to get themselves bailed out.

However, most of the new capital is going to pay off the old debt (or pay interest on it). If that's the case, the *company* isn't bailing out—it's sinking even deeper. For investors it amounts to throwing good money after bad. Watch out for companies with big, old debts.

5. Is There a Market for the Product?
Most prospectuses will give some indication of the market potential for the product. I use common sense here. I look to see if I personally would find the product useful. Then I look at market share. Is this the only company in the field? Or is it bucking big competition?

6. Finally, I Look to Risks.
I put risks last because they are so hard to evaluate in a prospectus. Remember, the nature of a prospectus is to divulge information. Therefore, as part of the disclosure process, almost every company will list every possible risk that could happen.

The list is frequently very long and very scary. And because everything imaginable that could happen is put in, it's hard to judge which risks are realistic and which are unlikely.

Quite frankly, when we get to the risk portion of the prospectus, I feel it's time for professional help. Unless I'm an expert in the field, there's no way I can evaluate the true business risks. It's at this point that a good underwriter and broker can step in and provide both cautions and assurances where needed.

THE BOTTOM LINE

This, then, is the order in which I read a prospectus. But please note that my list of items to examine is neither comprehensive nor complete. There are literally dozens of other items to carefully consider. As you develop your own techniques for reading a prospectus, undoubtedly there will be different clues that you will look for.

The only unswervable advice I can give is to DEFINITELY READ THE WHOLE PROSPECTUS. In many cases it is your first line of defense against a bogus offering. Just as it can be a confirmation of a really sizzling deal.

PITFALLS IN PENNIES

■

If you've come here looking for horror stories, you're going to be disappointed.

This chapter isn't aimed at scaring you away from penny stocks by telling you what terrible things were done to poor, innocent investors. It's been my experience in life and business that most of us get what we deserve. Or to put it as W. C. Fields used to, "You can't cheat an honest man."

If you go looking for bargains and ways to connive an advantage where none exists, be prepared to get your fingers burned. I'm here reminded of an investor I ran into who lost a great deal of money by buying gold bullion marked down 40 percent to wholesale prices. "Why," I told him, "there's no such thing as wholesale gold any more than there are wholesale dollar bills."

"I know," he nodded sorrowfully, "I know."

If you're over twelve years old, you should know that there are no real guarantees in life or business. You pay your money and you take your chance. In penny stocks the rewards tend to be greater, but so, too, tend to be the risks.

MINE FIELDS

Having thus noted that the greatest danger of all lies within, let's move on to point out that there are plenty of mine fields out there in penny stocks. The unwary investor can indeed get caught in a whole plethora of problems that he or she may never have suspected exist.

Most of these problems occur because this field is so speculative. Anytime there's the opportunity to make a huge profit, there are going to be those who try to siphon off part or all of that profit for themselves. Greed is always a great motivator.

Nevertheless, what we're going to be discussing should not be taken as true of the majority of the industry. Most brokers, houses, and dealers try to be reputable. However, in any field there are always going to be a few bad apples, a few who try to take advantage of investors. What we're concerned with here is to point out the pitfalls of dealing with the latter group.

NOTE: THE EXAMPLES IN THIS CHAPTER ARE NOT REFLECTIVE OF ANY PARTICULAR PERSON OR COMPANY. RATHER, THEY ARE GIVEN TO ILLUSTRATE PROBLEMS THAT HAVE EXISTED IN THIS FIELD AT ONE TIME OR ANOTHER. THE READER SHOULD BE AWARE THAT NO ATTEMPT IS MADE HERE TO BE COMPLETE OR COMPREHENSIVE. AS THIS IS BEING WRITTEN, NEW PITFALLS MAY BE ARISING. NO ASSURANCE IS GIVEN THAT BY AVOIDING THE PROBLEMS LISTED HERE, YOU WILL BE SUCCESSFUL IN A PENNY STOCK INVESTMENT.

THE BROKER WHO REFUSES TO SELL

Perhaps this should come under the chapter on brokers; however, I have listened to so many people complain about this that it must surely be considered a pitfall, and a prime one.

As you should know by now, having read the previous chapters, timeliness is critical in this field. Frequently making a profit depends on getting in early and then getting out before the stock stops sizzling.

But what if you can't get out when you want to? What if your broker refuses to sell your stock? It could mean a loss for you.

Would a broker really refuse to sell a stock (and reap a commission?)

Remember, we're dealing with low-priced stocks in a thin market. Frequently the brokerage house is responsible for keeping up the market for the stock. If many investors want to sell, then the stock will tend to drift down in price. That could mean a loss for the brokerage house.

Although it is illegal for a brokerage house to tell its brokers not to allow investors to sell a stock in order to artificially keep the price up, it is possible for houses to make it plain to their brokers that they will be unhappy about such sales. There are many ways they can do this. For example, instead of honoring the sell order, the house can tell the broker to "cross stocks."

The Broker Who Tries to Cross Stocks.

"Crossing stock" means finding an investor who wants to buy a seller's stock within a house instead of going to the house for the sale. Mr. Jones wants to sell; Ms. Smith wants to buy. They both are trading with the same brokerage house, so an exchange is made. This can save each of them as much as 10 percent on commissions.

In an active market, there's nothing wrong with this as buyers and sellers are going to be constantly in the market within a brokerage house. But sometimes the market is inactive; the stock is so thinly traded that there are no buyers, only sellers, so no crossing of stock can take place. Consequently your broker sits on your order, waiting. And your stock doesn't get sold.

The broker is under pressure from two sides. You want to sell, the house doesn't want to buy. Often the investor offers the least pressure. (After all, if the broker doesn't produce the way the house wants, he or she will soon be looking for a new job.)

Thus, when you go to sell, the broker may repeatedly find "reasons" (excuses) why it would be better for you to hang on to the stock. When you bring up the subject of selling, the broker may note that the company is about to make a new announcement that will favorably affect the stock's price. Or that he or she has heard something from reliable sources indicating that the price is about to take off.

If this happens again and again every time you bring up the subject of selling over a period of a month or more, you should begin to suspect that the broker has other motives for wanting you to hang on to the stock. If that's the case and you can't sell, you've just lost your leverage (your liquidity) in the market and you are in grave jeopardy of losing your investment.

What should you do? Of course, this usually only happens to beginning investors. An experienced investor who suspects such finagling will immediately order the broker to sell and give a time limit of a few hours. If the sale isn't completed, the investor will threaten to take the matter to

NASD and/or the SEC. Such action usually produces the desired response—a sale.

Of course, you may have ruined your rapport with your broker and may need to shop around for another one. But then, you'd probably be better off without the one you had, anyway.

THE UNCONSCIONABLE SPREAD

As we know, the spread is the difference between the ask, or what the house wants to sell a stock for, and the bid, which is what the house is willing to buy a stock for. For example, if the ask is fifteen cents and the bid is twelve cents, the spread is three cents.

But who determines the spread?

In penny stocks it is the market maker, the house. The house determines just how much of a spread it needs in order to cover its risk of stocking inventory.

Typically a brokerage house will want a large spread because low-priced stock is so thinly traded. With the value of total shares outstanding often less than $1 million, the house needs to protect itself against a sudden drop in price caused by a few large investors deciding to sell.

But how large a spread is justifiable? I have seen spreads where the ask is eleven cents and the bid is six cents. The spread is five cents, or almost 50 percent of the ask! If you buy the stock at eleven cents, it has to go up a nickel in price (almost 50 percent) before you could sell back and just break even. Is this justifiable? Is it conscionable?

Probably not. The house does have its risks, but sometimes it exaggerates them in order to make a killing on the spread. Sometimes houses may prefer to handle low-priced stocks mainly because they can get so much higher a spread (percentagewise) than they can with higher-priced stocks.

What to do? Here's a rule of thumb to follow that a broker friend, Dr. Bob Kirk, suggests:

When the stock is between zero and twenty-five cents, the spread should be three cents or less. If the spread is any higher, then the market may be too thin for you to consider.

When the stock is between twenty-five cents and a dollar, the spread should be six cents or less.

BE CAREFUL WHEN YOU BUY STOCKS ON THE PINKS

Remember, stocks that are not on NASDAQ are usually quoted on the pink sheets. However, the market here can be treacherous. When a stock is on NASDAQ, there usually is a retail price to which the market maker commits itself.

However, when a stock is on the pink sheets, the market maker is dealing with a very thin market and frequently can adjust the price without notice. For example, the pink might have one bid/ask quoted. However, if you want to sell a big order of stock, you may suddenly find that the bid drops 25 percent!

How come? The market maker didn't want to risk acquiring a larger inventory in such a thin market, so is decreasing its exposure. You, on the other hand, may find that you suddenly can't sell for the profit you anticipated.

There's nothing wrong with this, as long as you understand the risk. Be careful when you buy stocks on the pinks. A good thing to look for when buying stocks on the pinks is a narrow spread. A narrow spread tends to indicate an active and large market, one in which you have a better chance of selling without this problem occuring.

BEWARE THE COMPANY LINE WHEN BUYING

It's important that you, as an investor, understand the relationship your broker has with the brokerage house for which he or she works. Your broker is a "producer" in the eyes of the house. Your broker's job is to find investors who will buy stock, thus generating commissions for the broker and the house. Indirectly your broker's job also is to promote the stock the company is selling.

Thus, when you have a private, confidential conversation with your broker and he or she suggests you buy this or that stock, who's really talking? Is it the broker's best judgment in looking out for you, the client? Or is the company speaking?

In the past a few houses ran broker mills. They would hire new brokers, indoctrinate them with the company line, offer high commissions, and then send them out to find investors. These brokers would use high pressure tactics to get investors to put up funds.

When it worked out and the investors made money, everyone was happy. But too often things didn't work out. For a few months the new brokers might make big, *big* commissions, but then the hens came home to roost. Their investors were losing money, so they dropped the broker and, unfortunately, also the field. Suddenly these brokers couldn't find more investors. Their production went down and the house didn't need or want them anymore. They left and a new set of brokers was hired to repeat the process. Along the way, it was the investor who got hurt.

What to do? Find a good broker. He or she may not always belong to the largest firm. But be sure that your broker has done his or her homework. When a stock is touted, be sure it's the broker speaking, not the house. (We'll see how in the next chapter.)

CHURNING

This is the oldest trick in the book and the most obvious. Yet, since it still happens, it's worth mentioning.

A broker is supposed to look out for the interests of his or her clients. But just how the broker does the job is open to wide interpretation.

For example, I have a doctor friend who invested $50,000 in low-priced stocks this year. Thus far he has been involved in over 100 trades and has lost in excess of $26,000. His broker, however, has made a fortune on commissions.

My doctor friend told the broker something like, put me in the market, buy and sell as needed, and let's make some money. The broker interpreted this to mean something like, I'll move this guy in and out of the market as often as I can to make commissions.

The broker churned the account. The doctor is very unhappy. But if you asked the broker, she would probably respond, "It's just the risks of the market."

Since frequent buying and selling is typical of the low-priced stock market, it would be hard to prove the broker wrong.

How to avoid churning? That's simple. Number one, get a scrupulously honest broker, one who is interested in earning a living by making money for the clients, not by living off the client's money.

Number two, take an interest in what's happening. Like it or not, if you don't personally get involved in the penny stock market, you stand an excellent chance of getting burned. This is not an absentee field. You need to devote your time and energy to it in order to succeed.

WATCH OUT FOR PACKAGING

Thus far we've been concerned with broker and house problems. Now let's move on to other areas. This pitfall relates to new issues. It comes about because new issues can be hard to get, particularly when everyone wants them.

When the market for new issues is tight, some brokers may offer "packages." Yes, they can get you the stock you want, *but only* if you buy another stock they are selling as well. In other words, you need to buy a package. No, it's not legitimate, but it sometimes happens.

Many investors are so determined to get a new issue that they will go along. They reason, "So what if I buy a second stock. At least I'll get the new issue I want, which I'm sure will be a winner, and it will make up for any loss I might have on the second stock."

Such reasoning is simply fallacious. Not all new issues are winners. Even if a new issue is a winner, it may not be able to make up for losses on a big loser that was packaged with it. When you buy a package, almost always you significantly decrease your chance of success.

What to do? Experienced investors simply won't buy packages. They know that if they can't get one new issue, they'll be able to get another. There are *always* more coming out.

SHELL GAMES

A "shell" is a phony company that only looks like it's viable. The outside looks great, the inside is hollow.

A shell is made, not born. It occurs something like this. A company is formed with a dream. However, for one reason or another the product turns out to be unsuccessful. The company is a failure. Eventually there are a lot of shareholders, but very few assets. The company is not yet in bankruptcy, but it's getting close.

Promoters look for just such companies. They pick up the company for next to nothing. Now they own it.

Next the promoters go looking for a second company. This one has some sizzle—perhaps it's in mining or robotics or whatever happens to be catching investors' interests at the time.

The promoters buy the second company and merge the stock from the newly failed company with it. Now we have a shell, a company that superficially looks good because of the sizzle. But there's already a lot of existing stock out there free-floating.

Now we, as investors, come along and, because of hype and promotion by the promoters, are encouraged to buy the company's stock. On the surface, the purchase may look good.

However, we are actually buying stock at a high price that the promoters got for virtually nothing. (Remember, when they took over that nearly failed company for a song, they got a lot of stock for almost nothing.) In effect, we are buying "insider's" stock.

(Insider's stock is stock held by officers and directors of a company. Also called "Rule 144" stock, to protect outside investors it normally cannot be sold for at least two years.)

Eventually, when the promoters have sold all of the stock they can, the company has a "sudden" reversal. The promoters abandon it, it goes bankrupt, and we, as outside investors, have lost all our money.

How do we avoid shells?

There are a variety of things to watch out for. First of all, investigate all companies *before* you buy. If you discover through your investigation that the company was *recently reorganized,* be wary. If it was *recently reorganized with new management,* be doubly wary. There may be nothing wrong here, but it could be a shell game.

In addition, scrutinize the annual and quarterly reports. You can frequently tell a shell because it has little to no asset base. The book value of the stock is virtually zero.

Finally, if it has no NASDAQ listing, question why. If it's because there aren't enough stockholders to qualify for listing (remember, the promoters bought up the stock), it may be a shell.

The shell game seems to be played primarily out of the West. But it could occur anywhere, anytime. In this case watchfulness is what could save you from a fall.

THE RULES ARE DIFFERENT IN VANCOUVER

We mentioned the Vancouver market earlier. It specializes in gold mining stocks. There are some excellent opportunities up there. Unfortunately, there are also some rip-off deals.

If you're interested in playing the Vancouver market, you must realize at the outset that the rules are different. The SEC does *not* clear Canadian stock. There are other important differences as well.

For example, in Canada insiders are allowed to sell their shares much sooner than they are in the United States. Sometimes this leads to situations where they sell on opening day. Because this tends to be a thin market, this can skew a stock's price wildly up or down, misleading investors into thinking there's a lot of activity.

Also, in Vancouver a great many of the mining stocks can be only claims, not actual *producing* mines.

Finally, in Vancouver the investors are allowed to "short" their stocks, or sell stock before they buy it. (There's a more detailed explanation of shorting later in this chapter.) This adds a great deal of volatility to the market.

It's the old story of, "When in Rome, do as the Romans do." When you're playing the Canadian market, spend the time to learn the rules there. Or don't get involved.

DON'T OVERLOOK THE ADVISORIES

No one, not even full-time stockbrokers, has the energy or the time to check out all the stock opportunities. Most don't have the time to check out even 10 percent of them. Many don't have the time to check out 1 percent.

If this is true, then there may be a lot of bargains out there that we all could be missing.

To find these choice deals, I suggest you do not overlook the advisories (see Chapter 5). The advisories are not a panacea. Too often the adviser might be touting a stock that he or she owns. However, they are an excellent starting point for investigation.

WATCH OUT FOR "STALE" ISSUES

As we've noted, there is a certain time limit, usually ninetv days, during which the underwriter must sell new issue stock. If a minimum number of shares haven't been sold by that time, no stock can be issued.

One way to judge the popularity of a new issue is to ask how much time is left before the end of the sales period. If there's very little time left, a week or two, and the broker is desperately trying to get you to buy the stock, that tells you that for one reason or another, the sale isn't going well. There really isn't a whole lot of demand for the stock. All of which suggests it might not do well in the after market.

On the other hand, if there are still several months to run in the sales period and your broker is having all kinds of trouble getting it for you (assuming you have a competent broker), it suggests the stock is sizzling and may do very well in the after market.

The rule here is to beware of stale issues.

NEW ISSUE UNDERWRITER PROBLEMS

For the remainder of this chapter we'll concentrate on a specific group of pitfalls, namely those that have to do with the underwriters of new issues. Remember, we're not talking about most underwriters here, just those few who are out to take advantage of the investor.

We've already touched on some of these. However, now we'll expand and dig deeper.

1. Underwriting Mills.

Some brokerage houses have discovered a quick way to make easy money. Come out with new issues as often as possible.

When the market is sizzling, investors scramble to get

those new issues, so these brokerage houses feel they are just serving a need. However, a question of quality and service arises.

A house is expected to thoroughly investigate a company and only underwrite new issues of quality. But if the house is bringing out new issues almost every other week, just how much investigation can it possibly have done?

Additionally, the house is expected to service the new issue, that is, to not only promote it, but to support it through its first year. If the house is grinding out the new issues, does it have the ability to support all of them? Or will it be stretched too thin?

Be alert for brokerage houses that in reality are just underwriting mills. When a house comes out with new issues every few weeks, insist on seeing a track record going back several years. See how well the house supported stocks it brought out twelve months and eighteen months ago—not just the stocks that happened to do well, but *all* of them.

You may find a graveyard of failed companies.

2. Weak Muscles.

Be sure the underwriter isn't biting off more than it can chew. Every brokerage house wants to be an underwriter. Some can handle it, some can't.

Critical things to look for are how many offices the house has, how many brokers it has working for it, how much of the deal it is syndicating with others (and how much muscle they have).

However, perhaps the best way to judge the muscle of an underwriter is to look at the levels at which its previous three underwritings were stabilized. Remember, it's up to the underwriter to support the stock in the after market. How well the underwriter did in this capacity in the past is a good indicator of how well it will do in the future. If its last three issues quickly dropped off in price, is there much hope for the next?

3. Strong Muscles.

This is just the opposite sort of problem. Here we're dealing with an underwriter that is very strong. The underwriter has a lot of capital behind it. It may come out with a new issue and keep it entirely in-house. The idea is that the underwriter will use its muscle to retail the issue, at the same time controlling the supply. However, in such a case, how does the investor really know what the stock is worth?

After all, in such a thin market the price of the stock may not really be determined by investor demand, but instead by the underwriter. Since the house controls the supply (having bought up all the outstanding shares), it is in effect supporting the stock's price. It may be bid thirty cents/ask thirty-six. But the quote might be artificial, held up entirely by the underwriter's muscle. Since no other houses have it, it shouldn't be that hard to support the price.

Maybe the underwriter will support the stock for six months or so. But if it doesn't take off on its own, the underwriter's patience may diminish (particularly when income from commissions and sales diminishes) and it may let it go. Since the stock was probably overpriced to begin with, when the house stops supporting it, it tends to drop right off in value. The stock could suddenly plummet.

How do we avoid getting muscled by a house? The thing to do is to be alert for new issues that have these three things in common:

1. *Small amounts,* particularly in the $500,000 range and under. (The smaller the issue, the easier for the house to control the supply.)

2. Strong house.
3. No syndication—the only market maker from whom you can buy the stock is the house.

Of course, just because a stock has these three characteristics doesn't mean it's being muscled. But it's something to consider, particularly if in the past the house handled stock similarly and it went up dramatically in price, perhaps by factors of three and four, and then, after a few months, came down just as quickly.

4. Syndication Troubles.
The fact that a stock is syndicated is no guarantee of its success. Yes, syndication does spread the stock around to other brokers and other houses. But will they promote it? Is the original underwriter big enough and respected enough to command their support?

Be careful when you are asked to buy a stock and are assured of its doing well mainly because it is in syndication. This fact alone does not mean things will work out well in the end.

5. The Greedy House.
This refers to a sort of cycle that sometimes occurs in the market. Often there is every intention of doing a good job. It's just a matter of trying to get too big too fast.

Sometimes an underwriter will have particularly good luck with one or two issues. Investors will note what's happened and will come swarming in. The house will put on more brokers and business will be booming.

But to keep things going, the house needs more stock. So it comes out with several new issues. However, for one reason or another, these new issues aren't as attractive as the previous ones. The house suddenly finds that it has to support a lot more stock than it anticipated.

The house gets spread too thin. It can't support the stock and prices begin to fall. Its brokers get disgusted and they begin to leave. Investors are disenchanted and sell orders pour in. Ultimately the house can't meet its capitalization requirements and it has to close its doors.

Be careful when dealing with houses that are in the process of expanding. It's a critical period. Yes, they might do very well. Or things might just go wrong for them . . . and for you.

6. Stepping Up an Issue.
This is a tricky concept, but an important one to understand. Here we have an underwriter that increases the price of a stock and makes a profit for its investors. It seems to be a good idea on the surface, but if you buy late, watch out.

Let's suppose the new issue is sold for ten cents a share and the house brings out the stock in the after market at a bid of twelve and an ask of nineteen. Note that this is an enormous spread, seven cents a share on a very low-priced stock.

Those who bought the new issue obviously bought in at ten cents. The house brokers are encouraged to get these individuals to sell; after all, they will be making a two-cent profit (before commission, which may absorb most of their profit) on their sales.

At the same time, the brokers are encouraged to sell the stock to new investors at nineteen. The house uses its PR muscle and sales force to move the stock. It also sells at less than the stated ask price to those who buy bigger blocks.

The intention is to sell everybody out of the market who bought originally at ten cents. Eventually all the holders of the stock will have bought in at a stepped-up level, say fifteen or sixteen cents. Now the price of the stock can be moved up to, say, a bid of sixteen cents and an ask of twenty-three cents.

The idea here is that since no investors are into the stock for less than about sixteen cents, there's no downside risk to the underwriter. No one will want to sell and they won't have to take in any inventory.

On the other hand, the stock appears to be performing well. It's moved up substantially from its new issue price. And there are lots of happy investors along the way.

If it turns out that the stock has a little steak along with the sizzle, the underwriter may try stepping it up a second time, or a third.

However, eventually reality has a way of popping holes in the bubble. Sooner or later the stock has to prove itself. If it can, then of course the sky is the limit. But too often what we're dealing with is hot air, nothing but sizzle.

When disenchantment sets in

For one reason or another (usually no upward price momentum), after two or three months investors begin becoming disenchanted with the stock. One day there is "net selling" (more sales than purchases). Now it's up to the underwriter to support the stock.

However, the underwriter may be satisfied with the large commissions and profits it has already made. It may simply let the stock find its own level. It may allow demand to lower the bid price.

Lowering the bid price may alarm some investors, who will want to get out before a crash. They will want to sell before the price drops down below what they paid. In a very short time the stock could plummet to below the original ten-cent offering.

Timing is everything

As I noted, if you get in and out early, you can actually make some money on stock that is stepped-up. On the other hand, if you're the last one on the list, you could take a beating.

My guess is that no underwriter would admit to stepping up a stock, and the vast majority don't do it. However, occasionally it may happen.

The tip-off that a stock is being stepped up can be a huge differential between the bid and ask prices. Of course, this could also simply indicate a prudent underwriter protecting itself. Ultimately, probably the best way to avoid such a situation goes back to checking the track record of the underwriter. What's happened to *all* the stocks the company has come out with in the past six months to a year? Have some produced the pattern described here? If so, be careful.

7. Shorting Your Own Issue.

This is never supposed to happen. However, in any business there are always a few unscrupulous people. It goes like this.

The house is also a dealer. It maintains its own internal account. It can buy and sell stock for itself. But it has one big advantage over investors, particularly when it is stepping up a stock or muscling it or doing something similar. It knows when it's going to stop supporting the issue. It knows when the price is going to fall.

The underwriter can benefit from this knowledge by shorting the stock. Shorting, as indicated earlier in this chapter, is simply reversing the time order of a transaction. In normal time we buy first and sell later. When shorting, we sell first and buy later. Normally we want the price to go up; we buy low and then sell high. When shorting, we want the price to go down. We sell high and then buy low.

The actual mechanics of shorting involve making a commitment to sell and borrowing the stock from someone who already owns it. For example, the house "borrows" the stock from other houses, brokers, or investors and sells it at twenty-five cents a share.

The sale is really made to actual investors like you or me who are hoping it will go up in price. Now the house watches the stock drift down in price. When it reaches ten cents a share, it buys it (from investors such as us) and gives back the shares it originally borrowed. Along the way it's made itself a neat fifteen-cents-a-share profit (which we have lost).

Investors can short stock, too. There's nothing wrong with that. However, investors can only short those stocks on the "approved margin list." And this rarely includes penny stocks.

When the house shorts stock that it's underwriting, we have a definite no-no. (Note: some people understand shorting and others don't. If you're one of those who doesn't, simply believe that it does happen and watch out when the house does it.)

Detecting this is probably impossible for the average investor. Probably the only thing to do is to be careful with whom you do business.

THE BOTTOM LINE

We've discussed many things to watch out for, but I want to emphasize one particularly—track record. Before you become involved with any house or broker, ask for, insist, demand to be shown the *full* track record. Don't be satisfied to see just those issues that did well. See everything, every issue an underwriter has brought out. (If they don't want to show you, that tells you something, too.)

Remember, if you go back six months, a year, eighteen months, you may find a graveyard of failed companies. If you do, then the stock you are buying today may have a terminal illness.

Once again, I want to emphasize that what we are talking about here does not happen in the majority of cases. It's just a matter of a few bad apples in the barrel. You just want to be sure that you don't end up dealing with one of them.

FINDING A GOOD BROKER

■

Finding a good stockbroker, some have commented, is like Diogenes, the ancient Greek philosopher who reportedly walked the streets of his city with a lantern searching for an honest citizen.

I don't subscribe to quite such a cynical viewpoint. However, it is unquestionably true that it can be difficult to find just the right broker. After all, a stockbroker tends to combine aspects of an adviser, confessor, and confidant. It may take quite some searching before we turn up a person who can play these roles and with whom we can still feel comfortable. Adding to the difficulty are the problems that inherently are involved in a broker's position:

1. Conflicting interests

When we are in the stock market, we make our money from profits. A broker, on the other hand, presumably makes his or her money from commissions. We *only* make a profit when we have a successful transaction. The broker makes a commission *regardless* of whether or not our transaction was successful. In addition, the broker makes a commission each time we buy and sell. Thus, a broker makes a commission twice for each one time we can make a profit. This situation, of necessity, leads to conflicting interests.

Even when the broker is a totally honest individual (as most are), he or she must nevertheless feel motivated at some level to get us to buy or sell—or else, there's nothing in it for the broker. We, on the other hand, only want to buy or sell when there's a profit to be made. Thus, in the back of our minds there must always be the question, "Is the broker suggesting I make this move because it's in my best interests? Or is it because he or she needs a commission?"

When things don't go well, perhaps through no one's fault, it is only natural for us to question the motives of the broker. "Why did you get me into this transaction?" we demand.

It's hopeless for the broker to protest innocence. The inherent conflicting interest will always do him or her in. Ultimately the broker may throw up his hands and say, "It's your money. Do what you want!" In the fray a relationship can be severed and we can come away feeling cheated.

Some have suggested that to overcome this inherent problem in dealing with brokers, a new kind of commission structure be set up. The broker gets paid *only* a percentage of our profits. If it's 10 percent, then when we have a successful trade making, for example, a thousand dollars, the broker gets a hundred. On the other hand, if we don't make money or, what's worse, lose it, the broker gets nothing. This would tend to align broker motivation with our own.

However, for some reason, as of this writing I know of

no brokers who are jumping to adopt this new commission formula.

What is one to do, therefore? If you're a client, my suggestion is to be understanding. The broker does have to make a living, and if we only take up his or her time on the phone and never buy anything, that's a losing situation for that person.

On the other hand, we should also be prudent. If our broker moves us in and out of a lot of situations and we aren't making a profit along the way, he or she may simply be churning. In that case, it's definitely time to seek a new broker.

2. Broker inexperience

The title "stockbroker" tends to give an aura of professionalism to those who use it. In many cases the person is indeed a professional. Unfortunately, however, that's not always the case.

To become a broker, all one needs is a fairly reputable character and the ability to pass a less than awesome test. Having thus become a broker, one does not automatically also become a seer in the world of finance.

Typically a new broker is as awash in the world of stocks as is the new investor. When the two hook up together, likely as not it's a case of the blind leading the blind.

To overcome this problem, many brokerage firms these days offer their new brokers courses in stocks, bonds, and general finance. These courses are excellent, when they achieve their stated goals. Too often, however, the courses turn into sales meetings where, instead of financial knowledge, methods of manipulating the client are taught. Ultimately, for many brokers learning the ropes is done through hard trial and error.

It probably takes an individual broker with savvy between one and two years to learn the ins and outs of the market enough to be able to guide clients around the mine fields in penny stocks. Any less time than that and we as clients are in reality providing on-the-job training for the broker.

Therefore, a good rule with which to begin is this: If you're going to be investing your own money, never do it with a broker who's had less than about eighteen months direct experience in the field.

3. Compatibility

Finally, there is the matter of compatibility. I may be a daring investor, you a conservative one. Should we use the same broker? You may make quick decisions, I may take a long time. Will the same broker serve us equally well?

The point is that brokers have different styles. To be successful we need to find a broker whose style is compatible with our own. If, for example, we want to take a moderate approach, then we need a broker who is sympathetic to our needs and is a moderate him or herself. One who is radical and wants to take chances or who is too conservative will not fill our needs.

To find such a broker will take some searching. Just as you wouldn't want to be close friends with every person you'd meet on the street, you wouldn't want every broker to handle your money. We simply have to meet and talk with as large a number of brokers as possible before the right one will appear.

WHERE DO I FIND A PENNY STOCK BROKER?

If you want to find a broker who handles the Big Board, then any Smith Barney, Shearson, Merrill Lynch, etc. office will do. They are chock-full of brokers who will handle such transactions for you.

On the other hand, if you want to specialize in pennies, where are you going to find brokers? After all, most brokers handle only high-priced stocks.

There are sources, and we'll discuss them in a few paragraphs. But first, a word of explanation as to why this book does not contain a list of brokerage firms (if not brokers themselves).

My observation is that brokers move into and out of the field with amazing speed. Brokerage houses also seem to have relatively short life spans. Therefore, any list put into a tome that is long-term, such as this book, would probably be dated by the time it was in the bookstore. What's worse, a house "recommended" here could possibly turn sour in the future.

Thus, rather than provide you, the reader, with a list of brokerage houses and numbers to call, I am going to tell you where you can create a truly up-to-the-minute list for yourself.

It's easy. Chapter 5 contains a list of publications in this field. The larger of them, such as the *OTC Stock Journal* or the *Penny Stock Preview* or the *PennyStock News*, contain advertisements from brokerage houses specializing in the field. The house may be touting a new issue (asking you to send for a prospectus) or it may simply be promoting its services. In any event, from just a few copies of these publications you can put together a list of who's in the field as of the time you're searching. Then it's just a matter of calling around. (Many houses offer toll-free numbers.)

In addition, should this source fail, you may be able to contact some of the publications for a current list of brokers. They may have a recommended list they would be willing to share.

QUALIFYING A BROKER

Having thus commented in general on the broker/client relationship and where to find brokers, let's now turn our attention to the more specific subject of determining whether a broker knows what he or she is doing. Once we find a broker who we feel is fairly honest, experienced, and compatible, what else do we need to know? As it turns out, a great deal.

1. Is the Broker a Member of the NASD?

You'll recall from earlier chapters that the NASD is the self-regulating arm of the OTC market. *Any* broker with whom you deal should have, as a bare minimum, membership in the NASD. If the broker is not a member, then seriously reconsider doing business with him or her. (After all, if something goes wrong, with a member you can always threaten to take the problem to the NASD. If the broker isn't a NASD member, how much weight will your threat carry?)

Keep in mind that the NASD is a "voluntary" organization. Not every SEC-registered broker has to belong. The NASD provides an additional bit of assurance by conducting examinations of brokerage houses on a regular basis. The compliance department of the NASD will actually go to a brokerage house and examine records to see that SEC regulations are being enforced. Unfortunately, while this is helpful, it is still far from a guarantee that the house is completely honest.

2. How Long Has the Broker Been NASD Licensed?

This is a different question from the preceding one. If you ask about experience alone, the broker could answer,

"Several years." If you ask about NASD membership, the broker could answer, "Yes." But it could turn out that what was meant was that he or she has been slightly involved in the field as an investor for several years and got NASD membership yesterday.

A good rule of thumb is that the broker should be NASD licensed for at least eighteen months to two years.

3. Does the Broker Do His Or Her Own Research?

This is a critical point. In the last chapter we discussed the house line, where brokers would repeat information and suggest stocks that were given to them by the brokerage house. For obvious reasons (if they're not obvious, reread the last chapter), we want a broker who thinks for himself or herself, one who goes out and does his or her own homework.

There are several ways to determine if a broker knows his or her stuff. The first is to ask if the stock being recommended is being underwritten or a market made in it by the broker's house. If every stock the broker recommends is underwritten or a market made in it by his or her house, then you know you're getting a house line. The broker is simply recommending what the house wants to push. Time to look for a broker who thinks for himself.

Another way to check is to ask the broker for 10K and 10Q reports. The 10K is the annual, and the 10Q the quarterly report that a company must file with the SEC. They are the bread and butter of research. Any broker who is doing his or her own work will surely have checked into these.

I have a friend who handles new brokers with a little test regarding these reports. When he's dealing with a new broker who recommends a company, he immediately says, "Send me a copy of the latest 10K and 10Q reports."

"It's positively amazing," my friend says, "how many brokers suddenly stop in their tracks. One minute they're pushing a company on me, the next they're anxious to hang up and, I presume, get to work on the next pigeon. Of course, every once in a while I get lucky and a broker really does send me the reports. And frequently it turns out to be a very good recommendation and broker!"

Alternatively, it's possible to ask the broker about the reports over the phone. Questions about recent income, liabilities, debt, and so forth should be easily answered if the broker has read the 10K and 10Q reports and/or is looking at them. (Alternatively, the broker should be able to quickly get hold of the reports to get the answers.)

On the other hand, if the broker can't produce the information, then why is he or she recommending the stock? Is it because the house has said it's a good stock to push?

(Note: It should be understood that just because a house is pushing a stock does not mean it's a bad investment. It could be an excellent investment. What we are concerned with is finding a broker who gives equal diligence to investigating both the house line as well as outside stocks before making a recommendation.)

4. Beware of Brokers Who Rely on Technical Analysis Alone.

Sometimes when I ask a broker about the 10K or the 10Q reports, I get a very quick and sophisticated reply. "Don't worry about those," the broker says. "They are irrelevant."

"What's important to know," the broker may say, "is that this company is in a hot field and the product it has is sizzling. People are scrambling to get the stock. The price has been hitting new highs almost every week. You're just lucky I have some available, and you'd better act quickly!"

What the broker is really doing here is relying on a sort of technical analysis (discussed at length in Chapter 7). The broker has probably looked at stocks overall and made a determination as to what field is popular and what stock within the field is likely to be a hit. Then the broker is telling me that based on past experience, stocks with sizzle in a field that's popular tend to do well. So I'd better buy.

Well, maybe it could be a good opportunity, and what the broker says could be right. But how does one judge? If you haven't known and dealt with the person over a long period, how do you know that his or her judgment about what's sizzling and what's going to do well is right?

Remember, this isn't a field where you can easily give your money to someone else and say, "Make my fortune for me." Rather, you have to do some homework yourself. It's one thing if, based on your own research, you think a field and a stock sizzle. Maybe you'd be willing to play a stock based on this alone.

But when a broker gives you this kind of information, then you'd better ask for a little steak to go along with the sizzle. After all, a broker should be listening to more than just rumors and testing more than just popularity. He or she should also be searching for the good, solid, fundamental stocks that will grow. Turning up the stock with both immediate and future potential is the real benefit that a broker can provide.

If the broker is a technician alone, watch out. You might be better off getting your information at the local soothsayer's office.

5. Does the Broker Buy the Stock That He Or She Recommends?

For many of us, this is the acid test. We're sitting in a bar and a friend orders a drink for us that has a very weird name. When it arrives, it has smoke coming out of it, it's bubbling, and it's got a nasty odor. Our friend says, "Try it, you'll like it!"

We look at the drink and reply, "After you!"

What we're asking for is proof that it'll be good for us, that it will do us no harm. That proof takes the form of the other person taking the drink first. If our friend survives and smiles afterward, well then, maybe we will try it ourselves.

In ancient times kings would call their chefs out to personally taste the food that had been prepared to demonstrate that it wasn't poisoned. In the past the great researchers in medicine would frequently try out a new drug or treatment on themselves before risking it on a patient. Should we expect less from our stockbroker?

Look at it this way. You're in the market to make your fortune, right? Is your stockbroker in there for some totally different reason? No, he or she is out to get rich, too.

Thus, if a stock comes along that's really as good as he or she says, then your broker would be a fool not to buy it as well as recommend it to you. This is a truth that's solidly embedded in rock.

On the other hand, if your broker is recommending a stock but is unwilling to risk his or her money on it, should you? Would you take a medicine when the inventor wasn't willing to take it herself? Would you eat food that a chef wouldn't taste? Would you take a drink from a friend who wouldn't drink it himself?

Ideally the relationship you have with your broker should be one of mutual investing. You're both looking for a good deal. Your broker is out there finding them and making money two ways. The first is by buying stock. The second is by making commissions recommending that good stock to others. Anything less than this type of a relationship, and you should find another broker.

How do you know if the broker actually bought the stock? Ask to see a copy of his or her confirms, those little slips that verify a purchase. There's no reason in the world a broker would hesitate to send this to you, unless it didn't exist.

6. Is the Broker Too Busy for You?

In any house there will be one broker who's been around the longest, has the biggest clients, and is doing the best business. This is the broker with whom most of us want to deal.

However, this big producer may not want to take us on if we're starting out with a small amount of money to invest. He or she may already have several dozen clients who have hundreds of thousands of dollars to spend. Would this broker be as interested in us if we have five hundred dollars or a thousand?

This is a real problem when searching out a broker. Frequently we are ushered over to second (or third or fourth) best. While this "B" team broker we end up with may indeed have the time to spend with us, will he or she have the knowledge or experience to make us rich?

It's a common complaint and concern of new, small investors. Yet, upon examination it may prove to be unwarranted. If we go into a house, ask to see the manager, and then explain that we are a small investor, but that we plan to move up quickly and we want to deal only with the top producer in the house, we may very well get an entrée to the "A" broker.

Some top producers will take on all sincere investors, regardless of the size of their accounts. (Small investors can often recommend large investors to the broker.) If we don't insist on an unwarranted amount of time, make reasonable demands, and actively trade the market, we might very well get the attention of the top broker in the house.

Of course, if it doesn't work out this nicely, we can always try the next house.

It's important, however, that even after the first meeting, the broker continues not to be too busy for us. One sure way to check is to monitor the message direction. Are we always calling the broker? Are we always put on hold or told we'll be called back and then sometimes aren't? These are sure signs the broker doesn't have time for us. We shouldn't waste time with him or her, either, and should look elsewhere.

Ideally the message direction will be two way. The broker will call us with recommendations and suggestions as often as we call the broker. In addition, he or she should be sending us written materials on a regular basis so we can check out what's happening with particular stocks.

7. Does the Broker Have an Investment Philosophy?

While this may sound a bit esoteric, it can be very important. Both you and the broker should be operating on the same wavelength.

A good broker will begin a relationship by trying to find out as much as possible about you. She should ask whether you are interested in growth or just playing stocks. Long term or short? High risk or low risk? What is your personal market strategy? What fields do you prefer? What do you want to stay away from?

Armed with this information, the broker should explain her own philosophy. Does she prefer growth or playing? Long or short term? High risk or low? Does she have preferences in terms of fields and stocks? Does she play a "contrary" game? (Buy whatever the market says is bad?)

Now the two of you can stand off and look at each other. Are your philosophies compatible? If not, you'd better find a different broker.

8. Does the Broker Explain How Your Account Will Be Handled?

This, of course, includes how much the commissions will be, but it's much more. The broker should explain her method of operating. Many brokers simply recommend stocks and put you in. But they don't recommend when to get out. Ultimately, if the broker doesn't have a sound investment outlook, you could pick many winners and still end up losing money.

You can tell if a broker really knows how to handle your account if she gives you a "plan." Usually this takes the form of a counseling session at the beginning of your relationship.

The broker may explain that she will recommend stocks. If you buy one of her picks, at the time you buy the two of you will determine when you will sell if the stock goes down and when if it goes up. Thereafter, she will execute the plan for you. If the stock looks like it's going to be a real winner, she will call and ask if you want to change the plan and let the stock run instead of selling it.

A broker who is able to work out a plan with you demonstrates clear understanding of the market. A broker who simply says, "Let's buy!" and doesn't have an escape plan for selling may really be incapable of dealing with the market. Remember, the broker must do more than just pick the stock. He or she must also know how to get you successfully into and out of the market.

9. Does the Broker Have an Academic Degree?

Many investors would say, "Who cares if he has a master's or a Ph.D? What counts is, can he pick a winning stock!"

Indeed, that certainly is true. However, there's something about getting an academic degree that tends to instill a sense of respect for honest investigation in a person. Regardless of the field in which the degree was obtained (whether it be science or liberal arts), the degreed broker may tend to have a greater appreciation for true research.

Of course, that doesn't mean that a Ph.D. couldn't be an incompetent stockbroker. It's just that given a choice, I prefer to deal with someone who's waged the academic wars and succeeded than someone who has never been to that battle.

10. Does the Broker Have Connections?

This is important in a variety of ways. For example, if you are looking to play the new issue market, can your broker get new issues for you?

If you've explained what you want done and all you get from your broker are excuses, then perhaps it's time to consider a different broker. Some in the field simply don't have the connections to get the new issues. They don't know enough people, aren't respected by enough people.

The same holds true for growth stock. Some brokers have many connections in the field. A friend may tip them off about a great company. The broker may then research it and conclude it's a great buy and recommend it to you. But the whole chain might not have started without the broker's connection.

One way to check on a broker is to casually ask others in the field about him or her. Penny stocks is a small enough field that the top people tend to be known to others.

11. Can you Get a Friend to Recommend a Broker?

This can be an excellent place to start. I've put it toward the end of our list, however, because few of us tend to know others who are already involved in penny stocks.

Nevertheless, if you know an investor in the field, particularly one who's been around for a while and who's made some money, his or her recommendation of a broker can be invaluable.

12. Is the Broker's House Financially Sound?

They're all sound, you may think. Not so.

In terms of capital, all that a broker has to raise is a surprisingly small sum of money to open a house. For example, a house that is going to be a market maker could conceivably have less than fifty thousand dollars in net capital. (Net capital is net assets minus client indebtedness.) Of course, many houses have far more.

Nevertheless, the SEC requires that each house maintain a minimum amount of capital; this is called the "Net Capital Rule." When a house's capital drops below the minimum amount, the SEC may shut it down.

Shutdowns can and do occur because of insufficient net capital. They may occur for a variety of reasons. For example, the house may sell stock to an investor and then not receive the cash from that investor to make the purchase. The house has seven days to get the money. If it doesn't, then it is responsible for the money. This is called "Regulation T," and has been the undoing of some luckless houses.

In another instance a house might be shut down because it has speculated in the market and lost.

For whatever the reason, when a house is shut down, it means inconvenience at best and potential losses at worst. It could take weeks, perhaps months, to sort out the trades and ownership of stocks in a house that has been shut down. During that time you might be incapable of selling your stock.

It's important to ask your broker for a statement of the house's *current* financial condition. This statement should include a ratio of net capital to client indebtedness. The ratio can be any number, but if it's higher than eight (meaning the firm has less than one dollar for each eight dollars of client indebtedness), beware. Firms with ratios of ten or higher are getting into dangerous territory.

13. Who Is the Brokerage's Clearinghouse?

This question relates to the preceding one. Some brokerage houses clear their own accounts. Unless the house is very large, this is something to be wary of. (To see why, reread the previous section.)

Many houses, however, use other large firms to clear their transactions. Ask your broker what firm acts as the clearinghouse. Is that firm a member of the New York Stock Exchange?

The idea is to get a clearinghouse that's as big as possible. Remember, if the clearinghouse fails, as some have done in recent years, it can tie up your stocks for quite some time. On the other hand, if the clearinghouse is very large, a failure would cause such a market brouhaha that chances are the SEC would insist the mess be cleared up very quickly.

14. How to Interview Your Broker.

Thus far we have been looking at ways of qualifying a broker. Now let's try a different perspective. In a sense, getting a good broker is like hiring anyone else. We are going to be spending our money and we expect service in return. When we hire someone, we normally conduct an interview. The same should be true with a broker. We should interview him or her.

When you meet a new broker for the first time, whether on the phone or in person, you should have a series of questions to ask. Of course, you will form a general opinion by the way he or she acts and talks, but having those questions handy can help clear up matters quickly.

The actual questions you ask can vary enormously. I suggest you take a good number from those covered in this chapter. Just reword them to make them appropriate questions to ask a broker. For example, you can ask about the broker's affiliations, background, philosophy, and so forth.

In addition, to find out the broker's actual knowledge, sometimes it is useful to create a situation and ask what the broker would do. Perhaps it's something that has already happened to you in a stock transaction. You know how it actually came out. Does this broker have any suggestions or innovations that could have led to a more favorable resolution?

As personnel professionals know, the important thing when interviewing is to let the other person tálk. Your job is to listen.

With a stockbroker this shouldn't be too difficult, as most are experienced in conversing. The trick is keeping them on a topic of your choice (or else you may find they are already trying to get you interested in a particular stock).

Go through the questions in this chapter, but always keep in mind that what you are ultimately trying to do is establish a business relationship. That means that you don't "grind" or "grill" the broker to the point where he or she begins to personally resent you. That's hardly the basis of a working relationship.

Rather, be friendly, informal, businesslike. Point out that it's to both your advantages if you can learn as much as possible as quickly as possible about each other. And remember, the broker is supposed to be the expert, so don't try to show off what you know. Try to learn what he or she knows. (If you don't know something, admit it and ask for an explanation.)

Don't be in a hurry to buy

Ultimately, the broker wants to sell you stock. A good rule to follow is never buy on the first meeting (which should be when you interview the person). There are two reasons. First, you really won't know what you think of the person until after the meeting, when you've had a chance to think it over.

Afterward you may come to the conclusion that this broker is terrific and really knows his or her stuff. On the other hand, you may realize that the broker is all hot air and intimidation. If it's the former, then you can go back and start trading. If it's the latter and you've already bought, however, think how sad you may feel.

The second reason is that it's a good idea to begin with a trial period. If at the first meeting the broker recommended three different stocks, wait and watch those stocks for a few days or even a few weeks. If the stocks move up, that tells you something positive about the broker's ability to pick winners. On the other hand, if the stocks move down, it tells you something else.

If you wait, you can learn about the broker's abilities without actually spending your cash. If you don't wait, you'd better be an excellent judge from the starting gate or be able to sustain a loss.

Remember, you can almost always go back and buy later.

15. Ongoing Trial Period.

I once had a friend who had a rather self-centered attitude toward his job. Once when his boss indicated that he was unhappy about something in my friend's performance, this friend replied, "I was looking for a job when I found this one. I can always keep on looking!"

Regardless of whether his boss was justified in reproaching him, I believe my friend's attitude was sound and is worth considering in penny stocks. We're looking for a good broker. We may temporarily stop looking when we find someone who fits the bill. But as soon as a problem develops, we can keep right on looking.

Finding a broker should be an ongoing endeavor. We may start out with a trial period. We invest a small amount and see how well the broker handles the transactions.

If we're satisfied, we may want to stick with this broker a while longer and make bigger investments. If he or she picks good stocks, we'll hang in there. As long as we're making profits, it's going to be hard to change.

But there may come a time when profits turn to losses, when the broker makes a foolish error or two in handling a transaction, when there is a personality clash, when there is a question of honesty. What do we do then?

Why, we continue on with our search for the good broker.

Remember, unlike marriage, which is a very deep and personal commitment, hiring a broker is strictly a business arrangement. If we become dissatisfied with the broker for any reason and feel that the arrangement is no longer beneficial to us, then we can and should bail out. One of the biggest mistakes we can make is keeping a broker long after we've decided that he or she is not working for us.

SPECIALIZING IN MINING AND ENERGY STOCKS

The world of penny stocks is often divided up into different areas of interest. For example, there's high-tech stock and medical stock. But no field has received more attention recently than mining and energy stocks. These have become the darlings of investors.

Entire markets are devoted primarily to these issues. The Denver OTC market, for example, is widely known as the home of oil and gas stocks. Spokane frequently fields silver mining issues. Vancouver (unique in that it is a penny *auction* market) has literally thousands of gold mining stocks.

With all the interest in mining and energy stocks, it is little wonder that this is one of the first areas that new investors tend to explore. With the fever pitch of a forty-niner many buy the stocks in the hope of finding the miner's dream, a "glory hole."

But are there really fortunes to be made in mining and energy stocks? Is it really the easy way to get rich quick?

These and other questions are what we'll examine in this chapter.

TIED TO THE EARTH

Mining and oil and gas stocks are directly tied to the earth. This is the first rule of low-priced stocks in this field. If you buy a gold stock, then the price of your stock, in general, will reflect the price of gold. If gold goes up, all other things being equal, so, too, should the price of your issue. The same holds true for silver and for oil and gas. (There are other mining stocks, such as copper or nickel, but we're only going to cover the big three in this chapter.)

Thus, when judging the field, it is important to look to how well the product is doing on world markets. For example, as this is being written, all mining shares in general have been down for at least a year. Silver prices have been low. Gold prices have inched up only modestly, and oil prices have plummeted. (Gas prices have fared somewhat better, primarily due to long-term contracts.) As gold, silver, and oil go, so, too, go the stocks of companies that are involved in these fields.

But having low prices seems not to daunt those who are excited about this field. In fact, many feel that low prices mean prime time to invest in these stocks. It depends on your perspective. If you want to buy low, then when prices are down may indeed be the best time to buy. On the other hand, if you like to wait until you see a definite trend, then waiting until prices rise will probably make more sense to you.

Overall, however, the rule remains that the price of mining and energy issues reflects the price of gold, silver, or oil.

PICKING INDIVIDUAL SHARES

Having thus disposed of the market, what can be said for picking individual shares? There are two vastly different schools of thought here.

No Room for Amateurs.
The first school looks at mining and oil and gas stocks from a fundamental perspective. It states in brief that it is just as difficult to find a good mining or oil stock as it is to find a good mine or oil well.

In other words, this is a field *exclusively* for experts. It takes individuals with dozens of years of mineralogical and geological experience to be able to truly evaluate the potential of a company in this field, so how can investors expect to do it in a relatively short time?

This school points out that there are all kinds of pitfalls in trying to buy these stocks. From the out-and-out fraudulent promoter who is trying to sell "fool's gold" to the sincere oil well owner who, because of economic reasons, hasn't a chance, the field is littered with hopeless companies and worthless stocks. The novice would have a better chance of picking a winning ticket in a lottery than wandering in among these treacherous stocks and being successful.

Every Stock's a Winner!
Then there's the other school of thought, which says something to the effect that "it doesn't make a darn bit of difference what stock you buy. When the market's hot, everyone's a winner!"

This perspective pays close attention to the linkage described earlier between these stocks and the prices of gold, silver, and oil. When prices for the product are going up, according to this viewpoint, any stock in the field will do well, at least for the short term. Therefore, just jump in with both feet and get rich! (This viewpoint is most clearly presented in a book titled *Small Fortunes in Penny Gold Stocks,* by Norman Lamb, published by The Penny Mining Prospector, 1096D, Coast Village Road, Santa Barbara, CA 93108.)

Growth Vs. Playing.
These two viewpoints are similar to two other perspectives discussed earlier: buying a fundamentally strong stock for future growth versus playing with a stock hoping for short-term profits. As noted, it is possible to make money either way.

However, to my way of thinking, it is better to be selective when buying a stock. I like to know something about the company. I want to know that it has at least a realistic chance for long-term success. I want some steak with my sizzle.

Therefore, for the remainder of this chapter we'll focus in on some of the fundamentals that affect these stocks. If you want to take a fling at playing a stock and pick it just by throwing a dart at a board, go right ahead. There's really not much more to say except that before you do, you ought to read the last part of this chapter, which will give some insights into when gold, silver, and oil are likely to see better days.

However, if you want to see some of what you're up against fundamentally with these stocks, read on.

MINING FUNDAMENTALS

The fundamentals for gold and silver are similar. Therefore, rather than repeat ourselves, we'll take just one example, gold.

As the old saying goes, "Gold is where you find it." Today, however, locating an ore-producing body is not quite as hit-or-miss as it was in the past. Today geologists have sophisticated techniques for determining the likelihood of finding minerals underground. Unlike in the past, today knowing where the gold is can often be the *least* critical part of a successful mining venture.

To put it another way, while today mine owners usually have a pretty good idea of where the gold is, they are faced with other problems. These other problems can be lumped into two categories: (1) Is the known gold in sufficient purity to make it commercially worthwhile to mine? (2) Does the company have sufficient capital and expertise to start up production and become profitable?

IS IT COMMERCIALLY MINABLE?

This often separates the experts from the novices. Those who are promoting mines will often point to "proven reserves." They will indicate that their mining claims are right next to another mine that is commercially producing gold. Further, they may point out that their proven reserves may be quite large. The promoters may even have genuine geological reports substantiating the reserves.

Armed with these proven reserves, the promoters are out looking for capital. All that they need, they say, is enough money to start production. Buy their stock and join them on the road to riches. Should we buy their stock? Is it a good deal when a company has proven reserves?

Maybe. But the real question is not how much proven reserve a company has. It's how much of that reserve is commercial.

It works like this. Gold may be near the surface or deep underground. It may be present in very small quantities, or in strong concentrations. Obviously, gold that is near the surface in strong concentrations is going to be cheaper to mine than gold that is farther down and thinly spaced out. A company might indeed have, for example, $100 million in proven reserves. But that gold might be a thousand feet down and it might cost $400 an ounce to extract from the ground. If the current price of gold happens to be $350, then no way is this company going to be successful. If it started production, it would lose $50 on each ounce it produced.

Having commercial reserves means that a company has gold that it can extract from the ground for *less* than the current price of the metal. A good commercial reserve, for example, would be extractable at $275 an ounce when gold was selling for $325. A commercial reserve worth $2 million might be far more valuable than only a proven reserve worth $200 million.

NOTE: What's commercial and what isn't depends on the price of gold. A company that has gold extractable at $400 an ounce might not be able to sell its stock for a dime a share when gold is $350. But if the price of gold suddenly goes up to $500 an ounce, that company's proven reserves suddenly become commercially developable. That stock can explode in value overnight. Thus, even companies with only proven reserves can be sleepers, good buys waiting for the price of gold to take off.

Finding Out.

How do you know if the reserves of a company are commercially worthwhile or just proven?

The truth is that unless you're a geologist and a mining expert, you probably don't. This is one of the biggest problems with mining stocks. As investors, we usually only have the word of the mining company as to the nature of its reserves.

Sometimes respected outside experts are called in who render opinions, and this can be helpful. Sometimes newsletter writers spend time investigating particular companies and give opinions, and this, too, can be helpful. Nevertheless, the fact remains that the average nonexpert investor can never really know if a mine's reserves are commercial or not . . . until production starts up. This is an important fact to keep in mind.

DOES THE COMPANY HAVE THE EXPERTISE TO MINE THE MINERAL?

Who are gold miners? Remember back to the last century when half the East Coast went West to strike it rich in California? What did those people know about mining?

Next to nothing. And things haven't changed all that much today. Miners remain dreamers. They go out looking for a strike, sometimes hit it, and think that everyone lives happily ever after. Unfortunately, that's not the way it is in the real world.

It takes a fortune to make a fortune in mining. With gold, it takes enormous capital to start up a mine and get it into production. Yet very often those who are in start-up mining companies either ignore this fact or simply are unaware of it. It's easy to make the mistake.

Small-Time Mining.

Weekend miners sometimes do very well with suction rigs floating on rivers digging up placer gold. Small companies sometimes do very well simply by using a process called "leaching."

Basically, leaching involves just dumping the ore on the ground in a giant leach pit. Then a solution of cyanide is poured over it and this draws out the gold, which is then refined.

Leaching can make it possible for a small company to get started. For example, the *company* buys the rights to an old slag heap. These are tailings left over from mines that may have operated a hundred years ago. Back then the miners were unsophisticated in the ways of removing gold from ore. They let a lot of the gold escape to remain in the tailings.

The *company* starts with the tailings and builds a small leach field around them. Almost from day one the *company* may be showing a profit. The owners may think that mining is easy. Now they're ready for the big time. All they need to do now is to raise a little capital and expand their business. So they issue stock, raise capital, and are on their way.

For the unwary investors, however, this company could really be a Trojan horse. Once the company raises capital, what is it going to do next? The old slag tailings are limited. Where is it going to get the next ore from which to leach gold?

It's one thing for a company to set up a small leach field and show a profit on old tailings. It's quite different for that company to mine ore, set up a giant leach field, and extract gold. The latter requires expertise and huge amounts of capital.

When the small company tries to expand, too often it finds that it is grossly undercapitalized. It may resort to borrowing, quickly use up its funds, and then fold. The investors, of course, are out their funds.

Thus, new mining companies, the ones that issue low-priced stock, tend to be extremely risky. Even when the owners are honest and sincere, there's the problem of experience and knowledge.

How do we avoid this pitfall? It's difficult, but one way is to be very careful of new issue mining stocks. Looking for a company that has already locked in production from other than tailings and other than leach fields is another hint.

Finally, looking for a company that has a track record of several years is also helpful. The trick, of course, is to find such a company that also has a low price for its stock.

GETTING STARTED IN MINING STOCKS

If after seeing the two problems noted above (there are others as well), you are still interested in pursuing mining stocks, you should spend some time finding a broker who specializes in the field.

We noted that there are brokers who specialize in penny stocks. A subspecialty is the penny stock broker who only handles mining stock. He or she should be in a position to familiarize you with the field and to offer research on what's currently available. (Of course, here you should apply the same criteria noted in the last chapter, as for any broker.)

Calling around to various houses will put you on the track of mining specialty brokers. Checking with the newsletters and advisories can also be helpful.

The bottom line, however, is that if you want to be successful in mining stocks, rather than throwing a dart at a list of stocks, you have to learn the field. Figure on spending years, not just weeks or months, in this endeavor. Yes, it may take a long time, but the rewards could prove it well worthwhile.

THE MINING MARKETS

The Spokane market tends to be a hotbed of silver mining stocks. However, most significant new mining issues in gold come out of Vancouver.

The Vancouver market is unique in the penny stock field. It is a true auction market, with volume as high as forty million shares a day. However, unlike the Big Board or Amex or other American markets, this Canadian market lists stocks in cents. It is a true penny market.

It does not, however, abide by the same rules as do American markets. Remember, in Canada the SEC does not oversee what's happening.

The Vancouver market is known for high-flying and highly speculative issues. The prices are typically between twenty-five cents and fifty cents a share. (Anything below twenty-five cents often indicates a stock with problems, perhaps on the way out.)

The Vancouver market typically has about half a dozen new issues a week. This attracts many investors from both near and far. (Interestingly, it has been estimated that roughly 40 percent of the investors in Vancouver are from the United States!)

To buy a new issue from Vancouver, however, an investor is supposed to be a resident of British Columbia. Stocks are sold to those who have B.C. addresses or to B.C. corporations.

It's important to note that U.S. laws governing stock purchases and sales may apply to investors who purchase stocks in Canada. One consequence here may be a double tax liability. If a profit is made on stocks *in Canada,* the investor may potentially be liable for tax on the gain to both the Canadian and the American governments. As a result, some Canadian brokers will only deal with American investors who actually come to the broker's office in Canada and sign statements releasing the broker from any liability in the sale or purchase of stock.

Commissions for buying stock in the Vancouver market vary depending on what country you are in. If you use a U.S. broker, you can expect to pay between 5 and 10 percent. On the other hand, if you use a Canadian broker, the commission can be only 3.3 percent.

OIL AND GAS

If investing in mining stocks looked difficult, keep in mind that it's child's play compared to investing in oil and gas. There are several reasons why, but two are most compelling. First, most oil and gas companies look alike. They have exploratory wells, developmental wells, and producing wells.

Second, most of these energy companies are linked. Each company seems to own a share of a field or well with another company. The whole industry specializes in spreading the risk, as well as the profit, around. Therefore, how do you separate the good companies from those that will fail?

The Wildcatters.

Most small oil and gas companies are piloted by individuals who have been in oil and gas for a long time. They often have worked for others, gained experience, and are now going to try to make it on their own.

Typically these "wildcatters" will locate desirable land and then try to raise money to get leases on the land and to put in an exploratory well. They are looking for investors who are true gamblers. The reason is that perhaps three-fourths of all exploratory wells are dry holes. They either produce no oil or gas or what they produce is commercially undevelopable.

Many wildcatters, however, will spread the risk around. They will share their lease with others in similar situations in the form of partnerships. Thus, if any one partnership strikes it, they all do.

Risk sharing does help, but it hardly eliminates the chance of losing. The investor should be aware that this remains a highly speculative area.

Developmental Wells.

After exploratory wells come developmental wells. Although they are promoted as "less risky," they must be considered high-risk ventures.

Developmental wells are drilled to "prove out" an exploratory well that showed oil. They may be dug from land adjacent to the exploratory well.

While the name "developmental" suggests that the risk is less, more than half of all developmental wells prove to be dry holes. Just because one exploratory well is successful does not in any way guarantee that wells dug nearby will also be successful.

Lower down in the level of risk are those companies that have producing wells. These wells actually are pumping oil (or gas) and producing revenues. Companies with these types of wells tend to be more mature and their stock tends to be higher priced. Nevertheless, it's important to note that even here there can be important distinctions. A company can have, for example, fifty "gross" wells. It may seem like a substantial amount. However, because companies share risks, it may turn out that although it owns *part* of fifty wells, its ownership is equal to 100 percent of only three wells. Thus, this company only has three "net" wells.

Difficult Evaluation.

Although we've covered some of the parameters in whirlwind fashion, nevertheless we should be able to see that evaluating oil and gas companies has got to be difficult. While we can make some differentiation on the basis of exploratory versus developmental versus producing wells, this alone isn't going to help us come up with winners. Some of the best companies started out as wildcatters going for exploratory wells. Some of those that failed were companies with producing wells that tried to expand unsuccessfully or were poorly financed. Some of the more successful companies don't even do any work themselves, but instead buy pieces of other companies.

Just as with mining stocks, it takes an expert, someone who's directly involved in the field, to be able to do a realistic evaluation of a company. Again, finding a specialty broker and checking with newsletters and advisories will help. But ultimately, to succeed in picking good stocks, we're going to need to put in the time (sometimes years) to become our own expert.

THE PRICE LINKAGE

We noted earlier that the value of mining and energy stock is directly linked to gold, silver, and oil. As they go up in price, proven reserves become commercial, the profits of companies increase, and stock prices zoom. Thus, besides trying to pick the good companies from the bad, an investor in this area also needs to follow the price of metals and oil.

Interestingly, the prices of gold, silver, and oil are linked. They tend to rise or fall together. There hasn't been a time in recent memory when one was up while the other two were down.

Thus, the factors influencing them tend to be similar. Basically, what causes the prices of gold, silver, oil, and gas to fluctuate are supply and demand, inflation, and world crisis.

Here's how they work.

Supply and Demand.

Gold

Gold is supplied by over fifty countries worldwide, yet more than half of the entire new supply of gold comes from South Africa (roughly fourteen hundred metric tons per year). The world's second largest supplier is the Soviet Union, which sells upwards of four hundred metric tons per year.

Gold is very supply sensitive. Any major cut in supply tends to result in a significant increase in price. Thus, racial troubles in South Africa, which led to fears of mine closings, led to higher gold prices.

While most gold sales are relatively public, the Soviet Union tends to keep its selling clandestine. Thus, it is difficult to ascertain the effects of Soviet sales on the world market.

U.S. and Canadian producers of gold tend to be quite small, though growing. Mine production in both countries has been steadily rising since 1980.

On the supply side, gold is sensitive to the economy. The yellow metal's greatest use comes from jewelry. Since jewelry sales increase during economic expansion and contract during recessions, the well-being of the country is a strong factor in its price.

Other uses for gold include dentistry, electronics, and coinage.

When supply and demand are combined, we see that an expanding economy coupled with problems for South

Africa tend to be bullish for gold. Recessions and strong mine production tend to be bearish.

Silver

The tendency is to think of silver as a poor man's gold. Nothing, however, could be further from the truth. There is no single great supplier of new silver, as South Africa is for gold. Rather, dozens of countries produce silver. (Mexico is one of the largest producers.) In addition, silver is sometimes a by-product of other mining, such as nickel. Each year for the past several years, the amount of new silver mined has increased.

The supply of silver, however, is clouded by huge existing inventories. Since 1981 there has been an overabundance of silver, both domestically and abroad. Coupled with this immediate oversupply is an enormous overhang of "old" silver.

Old silver is metal, usually in the form of jewelry (previously this also included coins, but most silver coins have already been melted down), that comes onto the market whenever the price rises. India alone, for example, is reported to have some 300 million ounces readily available for melting and dumping whenever the price tends to go above seven dollars an ounce. (India has laws restricting the exportation of silver, but it nevertheless comes out in great quantities.)

As a result, there is enormous supply pressure to keep the price of silver low. On the other hand, there is relatively little demand pressure on silver.

Unlike gold, silver is primarily an industrial commodity. Its greatest use is in the photographic industry. However, with the advent of electronic video and fast film that uses less silver, this industry has cut back on its silver demand. Thus, while supplies of silver are large and increasing, demand is moving forward only modestly.

As a result, the price outlook of silver through the remainder of this decade remains clouded.

Oil

The 1970s was a period of oil shortage. OPEC (Oil Producing and Exporting Countries) effectively moved the price per barrel up from five dollars to nearly forty.

However, during the 1980s the oil-consuming countries significantly cut back on their demand for oil. This came about at the same time that many new oil sources (such as Alaska and Mexico) were brought on line.

As a result, the 1980s have proven to be a time of oil surplus. By 1985 OPEC's control over oil pricing had virtually disappeared and oil-producing countries were vying with each other for a diminished market. Saudi Arabia, the world's largest producer during 1984, kept production to less than 25 percent of its potential. During 1985 it moved up to 40 percent, still far below capacity.

Demand for oil is likely to remain relatively low through the remainder of this decade while supplies remain relatively plentiful. Thus, the outlook for a new oil shortage, unless caused by war, is not positive. Consequently, most experts are betting on low oil prices for some time to come.

Inflation.

Gold, silver, and oil prices are all related to inflation, but in different ways.

Gold and silver are reactors. They react to inflation. The reason is that they are seen as "hedges." Inflation means a loss of buying power for currency. A hedge is something that retains buying power. Gold and silver are perceived as having this power.

Thus, to hedge against rising inflation, investors buy gold and silver, and their prices move up, often rapidly. On the other hand, when inflation is low or declining, investors tend to stick the money in income-producing investments (which precious metals are not), and gold and silver prices tend likewise to go down.

Oil, on the other hand, is an affector. It affects the rate of inflation. The reason is quite simple—oil is used in the production of just about everything.

Besides directly affecting individuals at the gas pump, oil prices are factored into the costs of moving any commodity (whether by truck, rail, or plane) and producing any product (in the form of lighting and heating plants and operating machinery—and directly in many products, such as some fertilizers and plastics). Oil is ubiquitous in our society.

Thus, when oil prices rise, the price of just about everything else also goes up. When prices go up, we call it inflation. When oil prices go down and the cost of goods, thereby, drops, we call it disinflation.

An interesting sidelight to this is the fact that some monetarist economists refuse to recognize the direct relationship between oil and inflation. Rather, they feel that inflation is caused strictly by increases in the money supply without corresponding increases in productivity.

Thus, during the Reagan terms in office, the government's monetary policy was largely credited with reducing the rate of inflation. In reality, however, inflation was mainly brought down by a combination of falling oil prices and recession. (The lower oil prices allowed manufacturers to reduce costs; the recession prevented them from raising prices.)

World Crisis.

Finally, there is the matter of world crisis. This can directly and significantly affect gold, silver, and oil.

Oil is affected when the crisis centers around oil-producing countries. The war between Iran and Iraq, for example, produced important price jumps and slips, depending on how it went.

The war itself cut back production in both Iran and Iraq, thus keeping oil prices higher than they might otherwise have been. On the other hand, whenever the war tended to flare up and threatened to close the Strait of Hormuz, through which most of the Middle East's oil flows, the price of oil skyrocketed.

Similarly, any military or political crisis in any oil-producing country, from Saudi Arabia to Libya, is going to have a direct influence on world oil prices.

This will indirectly also influence the price of gold and silver. Remember, precious metal prices follow oil prices. While it might be months before an oil shortage produced any significant inflation, investors act on anticipation, and an immediate price hike in precious metal prices could be expected.

Additionally, gold (primarily) and silver (to a lesser degree) are seen as "coinage of last resort." In troubled times, when people are worried about war, they tend to convert their currency into bullion. It is for this reason that Middle Eastern investors tend to buy gold during crises in that part of the world. For the same reason, French farmers for generations have kept some gold coins hidden in the woodwork of their homes as a way of surviving during the repeated invasions of that country.

Though it's sad to note, political or military crisis in almost any part of the world is bullish for gold and, to a lesser degree, silver. On the other hand, periods of quiet tend to be bearish.

NOTE: Some so-called experts point to a so-called gold/silver relationship. They indicate that there is an almost mystical relationship between the two, which they frequently peg at around thirty to one (gold's price is thirty times that of silver). When the ratio is higher or lower, they then extrapolate that conditions are unstable and that the ratio will return to the thirty-to-one norm. Thus, when the relationship is high, investors should buy silver because it is underpriced. When it is low, they should buy gold because it is priced too low.

This is simply nonsense. Historically, the ratio between gold and silver has moved up and down enormously at different times. Only during one period, between the Great Depression and 1975, did the price tend to remain at roughly thirty to one for a long while. That, however, was because the government officially fixed the price of gold and unofficially determined the price of silver (by selling government hoards to keep prices artificially low). Prior to that time and since, there has been no historical "norm" for the ratio between gold and silver.

Yes, gold and silver do tend to move together. However, that is usually because they are influenced by similar fundamentals and because investors perceive a relationship between them, not because the two metals are in truth tied together in some magical manner.

THE BOTTOM LINE

Yes, there's plenty of money to be made by investing in mining and oil stocks. Unfortunately, there's also plenty of risk involved. The best advice, if you're determined to proceed, is to do so cautiously. Learn as much as you can and, until you become quite knowledgeable, invest as little as possible.

APPENDIX

■

National Association of Security Dealers
1735 K St. N.W.
Washington, D.C. 20006
202-728-8000

CRITERIA FOR INCLUSION IN QUOTATION LISTS

I. Composition of the Lists

There shall be two recommended lists of NASDAQ securities provided to the media: the "National List" and the "Additional List." Inclusion on the lists shall be determined semi-annually on the basis of information available to the Association on the selection date. All quotations released shall be Level I quotations.

II. National List

A. *Domestic Common Stock*

The financial criteria for domestic common stock are separated into two alternative categories detailed below. Issuers which meet either one of the alternative criteria will be included in the National List regardless of their dollar volume. Alternative No. 1 includes a net income requirement while Alternative No. 2 has no income requirement but establishes higher financial requirements for those development companies which have no operating income:

Alternative No. 1

1. 350,000 Publicly Held Shares
2. Market Value of Publicly Held Shares of $2,000,000
3. Minimum Bid Price of $3.00
4. Net Income of $300,000 in the previous fiscal year or in two of the last three fiscal years.

Alternative No. 2

1. 800,000 Publicly Held Shares
2. Market Value of Publicly Held Shares of $8,000,000
3. Net Worth of $8,000,000
4. Incorporated for 4 Years

B. *Foreign Securities*

Foreign issues and American Depository Receipts (ADRs) registered pursuant to Section 12(g) under the Securities Exchange Act of 1934, as well as issues for which all relevant information has been filed with the Securities and Exchange Commission pursuant to Rule 12g-3-2, shall meet the same criteria as domestic common stock except that the publicly held shares requirement for ADRs shall be determined by the number of ADRs outstanding.

C. *Warrants*
Common stock of issuer must be in the National List and all criteria for domestic common stock apply except that the publicly held shares requirement is replaced with 450,000 warrants publicly held at the time of the initial distribution.

D. *Convertible Debentures*
Common stock of issuer must be in the National List and $100 million of the issue must be outstanding.

E. *Units*
All criteria for domestic common stock apply except that the publicly held shares requirement is replaced with 350,000 publicly held units at time of initial distribution.

F. *Rights*
Automatically included if common stock of issuer is quoted in the National List.

G. *Preferred Stock, Shares or Certificates of Beneficial Interest of Trusts, Limited Partnership Interests, Real Estate Investment Trusts and Closed End Funds*
Same criteria as domestic common stock.

H. *New Issues*
Securities that meet the above criteria immediately following an initial distribution or secondary offering will be added to the National List on the day of the distribution.

III. Additional List

All positions in the Additional List will be filled on the basis of dollar value of average weekly volume.

To monitor security volume data in NASDAQ a statistical moving average method called exponential averaging is used and is recomputed weekly. This technique gives more weight to the most current volume and less weight to the most distant past. For example, at present the weighting parameter is chosen to give 10 percent weight to the most current volume and less than 1 percent weight to the volume that occurred 23 weeks ago. Thus, the significance of the reported volume as maintained for more than 6 months is virtually nil.

INDEX